ELECTRONIC
MEDIA
ETHICS

ELECTRONIC MEDIA ETHICS

Val E. Limburg

Edward R. Murrow School of Communication
Washington State University
Pullman, Washington

Focal Press
Boston • London

Focal Press is an imprint of Butterworth-Heinemann.

Copyright © 1994 by Butterworth-Heinemann
⊖ A member of the Reed Elsevier group.
All rights reserved.

Library of Congress Cataloging-in-Publication Data

Limburg, Val E.
    Electronic media ethics / Val Limburg.
      p. cm.
    ISBN 0–240–80145–8
      1. Mass media—United States—Moral and ethical aspects.
    I. Title.
P94.L56 1994   93-38124
174--dc20   CIP

British Library Cataloguing-in-Publication Data

A catalogue record for this book is available from the British Library.

Butterworth-Heinemann
313 Washington Street
Newton, MA 02158

10 9 8 7 6 5 4 3 2
Printed in the United States of America

Contents

8 ───────────────────────────────────────

9 ───────────────────────────────────────

10 ──────────────────────────────────────

Acknowledgments

A work of ethics is necessarily the product of a lifetime accrual of values. Thus, those values formed over the years in family, in religious experiences, and in associations with colleagues, students and professional broadcasters have formed the observations found in this work. In raising questions about our perceptions of ethics, perhaps my own way of seeing things becomes evident. Observations about the social context in which we make value judgments will reveal differences between generations; my sight may reflect the eyes of someone over fifty. In some cultures such age is proportionately related to "wisdom," a characteristic that is elusive, as are its applications in matters of ethics in telecommunications. Younger eyes, however, may more easily discern relevance.

Some insight has been lent me by professionals, among them Mark Allen, Pat Scott, and Steve West. They have demonstrated a concern for ethics as they make significant contributions in broadcasting.

Other help has come in the form of the expression of ideas. I am grateful to Marilyn Rash and the editing professionals of Butterworth–Heinemann, who have helped me with clarity of thought and effective style.

I am grateful to Alex Tan for his patience in granting me the time necessary to develop these writings, and to my colleagues and staff at the Murrow School of Communication for their ideas and contributions. Further insight and help have come from some healthy exchanges at the Poynter Institute for Media Studies, the Gannett Foundation (now the Freedom Forum), the Association for Education in Journalism and Mass Communication, the

National Association of Broadcasters, and the Broadcast Education Association.

Most of all, I am grateful for the day-to-day encouragement and support of my family. My companion, Jan, my children, and my grandchildren teach me something of what's really important in life: that in a world of cynicism and pseudo-sophistication, real joy can still be found with simple things.

October 1993

Introduction

For many years we have been seeing numbers that imply the penetrating influence of radio and television on American society. These media have influenced the way we use our time and the way we buy things, and they have set the tone for the most important values in our culture. Their power has surpassed that of every other American institution, including schools, churches, and even the family. They affect the way we see things, and the way we consume our fiction.[1]

- About 99 percent of all U.S. households now own a television set. Television sets outnumber refrigerators and even indoor plumbing in U.S. households. The average TV household views an estimated seven hours a day.
- An average preschooler watches five to six hours of television each day.
- By the age of 18, the average child will have watched 25,000 hours of television, more than any other single activity except sleep—including time spent in school, play, and time with parents. In that extensive viewing, such a child will have been impacted with 350,000 commercials, 15,000 violent deaths, and 7,000 "adult" or "mature" situations involving sexual predicaments.
- The average household has 5.5 radio sets; 95 percent of all automobiles have radios. Persons aged 12 and over spend 3 hours and 12 minutes daily with radio.

- The average adolescent listens to the radio for more than 40 hours per week. He or she may hear the same "current hit" song 60 times during that week.

In a *quantitative* way, television and radio form the *quality* of our lives.[2]

FROM NUMBERS TO VALUES

If radio and television are so popular from a numbers viewpoint, why is it that some observers see them as so bad? After all, these media give people what they want, don't they?

In our society numbers have come to be regarded as reality; a radio or TV show is "good" if it receives high ratings—that is, large numbers. Television and the pervasive culture it portrays have become reality for many people. But the meaning of such reality often goes unexamined.

We equate quantity with greatness, popularity with worth. The leap from making simple quantitative descriptions to making quality and value judgments is easy to make. We may go to great lengths to determine the accuracy of the numbers we have or the validity of a sampling or statistical measurement. Yet in analyzing what the numbers mean—in assessing the qualitative aspects of the situation—we are left without much basis for making broad objective judgments. You and I usually make judgments based on our personal values. Such is the stuff of which the great diversity of our society is made.

MEDIA VALUE SYSTEMS

This book studies the values portrayed in the media and how those values influence those of individuals. It explores the following questions:

1. Why explore this issue of values in the first place? The reasons for undertaking the examination are discussed in Chapter 1.
2. How have media values been formed historically? *Historical* examination can be done through *juxtaposition,* comparing the

specific practices, values, and styles of one era with those of another. We will examine the historical context from which radio and TV sprang in Chapter 2.

3. How does our use of the media determine our values about much of what we see in the world? The extent of our use really defines the people and settings around us. This is the topic of Chapter 3.

4. How do professional *codes* formed by industry leaders determine what is considered ethical in their professional conduct? These codes are often a mix of historical settings and current social mores, a situation discussed in Chapter 4. Also considered in this chapter are the narrower *standards and practices* that become established within individual organizations. Company handbooks and policy manuals that reflect these standards and practices may change as often as the executives who redirect company methods.

5. What is the specific content of radio and television programs? We examine the ideas being written by the creative community and exhibited by on-the-air personalities in Chapter 5 (radio) and Chapter 6 (television), so that they can be compared and contrasted with our own values.

6. Are there values contained in news broadcasts of which we are only dimly aware? Our view of the world that lies outside our own immediate domain, after all, comes to us almost entirely from the media. News carried over both radio and TV may set the tone for a day; it may alert us to dangers—physical, financial, or weather related. Its influence is examined in Chapter 7.

7. What are the economic overtones of the hundred-billion-dollar media advertising industry? The persuasive messages of advertising not only contain obvious values but also may contain subtler values of which we are only dimly aware. This issue is the subject of Chapter 8.

8. What are the subtle and obvious values of the economics of the business as they affect us all? The profit-oriented business base of the media gives radio, television, cable, and the newer telecommunications technologies their potential for greatness and influence, which is examined in Chapter 9.

9. Finally, what are some of the more positive, prosocial, and proactive values with which some of the industry is responding? Such approaches are examined in Chapter 10.

ARE THERE DEFINABLE MEDIA CONSUMER VALUES?

As adults sit down to watch television, they bring to the setting a vast array of values concerning issues of both media content and use. Younger TV viewers and radio listeners bring fewer values, but they are more likely to have their own values formed by the ideas of the media. But how do media consumers know just how much influence the media have had on their value systems? Good measurement is so difficult and puzzling that media users will likely have trouble intelligently sorting out and responding to the value systems portrayed in the media.

This book does not attempt to lay out what broadcast ethics "ought" to be. Rather, it seeks to allow the reader to be aware of as many perspectives on this issue as possible, including those that are less popular.

Do I take sides on the value conflicts presented here? The answer is yes—perhaps several sides, often on the same issue. With sometimes wild swings, I may seem to vacillate from one position to another, changing perspectives, looking at possible values from angles that may be new or different to the reader. Only by so doing, however, can there be intelligent examination of values and value conflicts associated with media assessment and the decision-making processes involved in many of the areas of the media. Emotions or affective concepts are, after all, difficult to assess and are rarely judged adequately or completely.

It may become apparent that a total vacuum of values is impossible; I hold to the notion that only a fool would claim to hold no opinion or have no values as he or she examines a value-laden situation. But be patient, dear reader, in sorting out the values.

ETHICS PLUS BROADCASTING EQUALS WHAT?

"What happens when you combine ethics with broadcasting?" runs a quip told by my colleagues in media criticism. "You get an oxymoron," I am told. Yet there is a great deal of interest today in examining the ethics side of this twentieth-century phenomenon. Why should there be so much interest? After all, isn't ethics something antiquated, carried over from the past?

Today we may have lost both our perspective on and our appreciation for ethics. Through many centuries, much of "scholarship" was devoted to the study of philosophy, including religion and mythology. Indeed, even today the highest formal degree bestowed in education is the Doctorate of Philosophy, or Ph.D., a degree that implies an understanding of the theory and wisdom behind a discipline.

In the nineteenth century, an ethics course was a keystone in the typical college curriculum. Students usually took the course in their senior year, and it focused them on how to think about the knowledge they had learned. This course was where *information* began to turn to *wisdom*, and it helped students understand how to use wisdom to become "better" or morally stronger people. As if to emphasize the importance of the ethics course, it was taught by the dean or even the president of the college.

It is worth noting that the old library classification system, the Dewey Decimal System, devised in 1876, divided the books that contain our knowledge into ten major categories. Out of a total of one thousand numbers, a hundred were devoted to philosophy and ethics. Another hundred were given over to religion and mythology, and a hundred each to philology (languages), social science, fine arts, literature, and history/geography. General works and technology each had a hundred, and all of science had only one hundred.

This hardly represents the distribution of emphasis on areas of knowledge as they are taught today in higher education. With the emergence of scores of new sciences, each with hundreds of studies within it, the Dewey Decimal System quickly became outmoded. A new classification system was developed that would better reflect the way we think about our newly acquired knowledge and that contained provisions to grow in whatever direction new information came.

In the meantime, the emphasis on both philosophy/ethics and religion/mythology shrank. By the mid-1960s, courses in ethics and moral philosophy began to disappear; so did some philosophy curricula. Most considerations of applied philosophy were now placed under "social problems" or "current events" labels. As the labels changed, so did our collective ability to reach back through the ages to the ancient Greeks and Romans and even to the nineteenth-century Germans. Some perspective was lost, and most of the guardians of our store of knowledge in higher education did not even spot the demise.

It should not be surprising, then, that a consideration of "ethics" in the twentieth-century influence of broadcasting on technology, business, and society does not seem to juxtapose very well. Still, as we near the close of the twentieth century, an interest in applied ethics is being renewed: courses in medical ethics, business ethics, ethics in government, and journalism ethics are now being offered. Indeed, within the last few years there has been a virtual explosion of ethics courses in journalism and mass communications curricula.

Nonetheless, a problem remains: Most such studies in mass communications fall within the domain of *journalism*, albeit both print and broadcast journalism. There has been little focus on the various other aspects of broadcasting and telecommunication. This work attempts to address that gap.

STUDYING THE ISSUES OF ETHICS IN BROADCASTING

There also has been a new interest in taking a closer look at the ways the creators, artists, programmers, journalists, and advertisers *encode* values, and in the ways media consumers *decode* them as they ponder what they have just consumed—often while their intellectual defenses are down. In other words, what are the broadcast media trying to tell us, and what are we understanding? This query has been addressed in a wide variety of formats, not only in the expanding interest in the study of media ethics in college curricula but in studies of media creators' value systems.[3] Consumer groups, too, are clamoring for more "responsible" behavior in the media.

Besides the news functions, there are other components of media that demand study in terms of ethics, such as the creative roles in programming or entertainment and the profit-oriented business role. The need for an evaluative examination of some of these other components has prompted the explorations and case studies for this book. Hopefully, it will serve as a text for media workers and managers, for students in media ethics, and for consumers who wish to give perspective to their interest in media values.

NOTES

1. For a full discussion of this issue, see C. Tichi, "Television and Recent American Fiction," *American Literary History* 1 (Spring 1989): 114–30.
2. A good discussion of this issue is found in Robert W. Kubey and Mihaly Csikszentmihalyi, *Television and the Quality of Life: How Viewing Shapes Everyday Experience* (Hillsdale, N.J.: Lawrence Erlbaum Associates, 1990).
3. S. Robert Lichter, Stanley Rothman, and Linda S. Lichter, *The Media Elite* (Bethesda, Md.: Adler and Adler, 1986).

1

Is There a Need for Broadcast Ethics?

In 1930, a radio station in Milford, Kansas, was licensed to one Dr. J. R. Brinkley, who went on to use the radio station to sell his packaged remedies. Brinkley was a "doctor" who would give "goat gland" operations to restore drooping vitality. Often, he would receive letters from patients with medical problems, and he would diagnose them over the air:

> [Here's a letter] from the Sunflower State, from Dresden, Kansas. Probably he has gallstones. No, I don't mean that. I mean kidney stones. My advice to you is to put him on Prescription No. 80 and 50 for men, also 64. I think that he will be a whole lot better. Also drink a lot of water.[1]

People in the medical profession regarded diagnosing ailments and prescribing "medicine" in this manner as highly unethical. The Federal Radio Commission, which oversaw broadcasting at that time, also felt that "Dr." Brinkley's behavior violated the trust he had been granted when given the right to broadcast over the public's airwaves. He had not broadcast in the "public's interest, convenience or necessity," the commission held. The practice was more than unethical—it was illegal. Dr. Brinkley lost his station's license to broadcast.

From the very beginning of broadcasting, through the generations until the present time, discussions, debates, and even battles have been waged over whether there should be qualitative standards in broadcasting. As radio evolved, so did detailed rules of professional ethics, guiding broadcasters as to what kinds of conduct were ethical. The most notable and nationally visible set of rules was the very detailed Code of Good Practice of the National Association of Broadcasters (NAB).

This code was dropped in 1982, however, leaving the industry without a national professional code of ethics for eight years. In 1990 the NAB articulated a new Statement of Principles of Radio and TV.[2] Even then, many broadcasters felt that it should be the *receivers* (listeners) who determined the ethics of what they chose to receive, rather than the *senders* (broadcasters), who would have to make moral decisions for the receiver—a kind of "value censorship."

Broadcasting standards were imposed from sources outside the profession as well. In passing the Communications Act of 1934, the U.S. Congress placed specific responsibilities on broadcasters, pointing to the need for them to exercise caution when broadcasting questionable materials. The act mandated the Federal Communications Commission (FCC) to ensure that broadcasters acted in the "public interest, convenience and necessity" in using the "public's airwaves."

Questions remained, however, as to whether there should be national standards, or whether each station should have its individual code. Today, the battle continues to rage on two fronts:

- whether to have articulated professional standards on a national level, and
- if there are to be standards, what they are and who is to determine them.

BRIDGING THE GAP: FROM CLASSICAL TO PROFESSIONAL ETHICS

At a recent National Radio Conference of the National Association of Broadcasters, I conducted a panel on ethics with the heads of several broadcast corporations. These figures gave mixed responses to the ethical dilemmas presented in various case studies on radio and television programming.

Here are some of the case studies they addressed. If you were a station manager or the head of a large broadcast corporation responsible for providing profit to the stockholders, how would you answer the questions they raise? (Do not look for the "right" answer to any of these cases—instead, use some of the philosophies that clarify the values by which you arrive at your answer.)

Case Study 1.1: Make a Profit, or Heed Community Voices?

You have a highly successful album-oriented rock (AOR) format in a medium market, and your morning disk jockey is the highest rated among all the stations there. Recently, a heavy metal rock group that receives a lot of play on your station was sued for allegedly encouraging suicide through subliminal messages in their song lyrics. Several community groups are threatening to picket your station and boycott your advertisers if you continue to play selections from the group's latest album. Your highest-rated popular morning jock, citing First Amendment rights, has threatened to quit if you bow to this pressure. You know that ignoring the pressure groups' concerns could cost the station considerable profit and perhaps put its license in jeopardy.

Which group do you side with in this dilemma?

Case Study 1.2: Listen to Advertiser or News Director?

As a TV station manager, you are caught between the conflicting demands of your news director and your sales manager. Your local news program has been running a series of reports on defects recently discovered in new Mazda autos. One of your best advertisers, a Mazda dealer, is protesting your station's airing of the series. "Take it off, or you lose my business," he demands. If you keep running it, you risk losing thousands of dollars' worth of badly needed advertising. Yet this series seems to be one of the more popular parts of the news. Your news director says keep the series going; do not let outside interests dictate news content. Your sales manager tells you that the Mazda dealer is a prize account—one of the biggest local advertisers. Whose voice do you heed?

Case Study 1.3: Make a Profit, or Respond to a Social Problem?

The music and format of your radio station generally attract a young audience, mostly teenagers. Traditionally, one of your best advertisers is the co-op advertising[3] of a beer company. Knowing the problems caused by teenage drinking—300 people killed each day in alcohol-related deaths, broken homes, alcoholism, and the like—not to speak of its illegality, you consider dropping the beer ads. But the revenues from such ads are what keeps the station financially in business. What should you do?

DEFINING ETHICS AND THE PROBLEM OF COMMONALITY

Could one reasonably expect that the value systems of a New York disk jockey, a news director, and a small-town radio station manager would be the same? Probably not. Yet the issue of common ground may be a logical place to begin our exploration of broadcast ethics. What are some of the definitions on which such diverse figures could potentially agree?

An overview of some terms, concepts, and definitions might serve as a starting point. Although it seems far afield from the day-to-day standards of a big-city disk jockey, the ancient Greeks actually classified *ethics* as one of three kinds of philosophy:

- *aesthetics,* the study of beauty;
- *epistemology,* the study of knowledge and how we learn; and
- *ethics,* the study of right or good conduct as it affects the individual (character) and society.

Ethics suggests sets of *values* by which judgments of good or right are made, or even the fabric of individual character. Ethics involves a whole system of sorting out values—good ones from bad ones, right ones from wrong ones, desirable or practical ones from unde-

sirable or impractical ones. They may actually be part of a philosophy—a personal philosophy, or a more general philosophy, perhaps one that has been recognized over a long period of time, or
one that has been articulated or debated by the greatest minds over
the centuries.

Choosing one value over another is thus the basic process that
constitutes a system of ethics. But what is a value? Generally, a
value is something that is of worth or merit or usefulness to the
person who is judging or evaluating. It is that which is considered
desirable and worthwhile—to be sought after and obtained. Values
may be individual in nature, like honesty, courage, and compassion. Or they may be social in nature, like freedom and justice.
Developing a set of values or a *value system* involves choosing or
prioritizing one value over another.

If we have a friend who is in trouble with the law, for example,
we may choose *compassion* and helping that friend over *loyalty* to
obeying the law and turning in that friend. We may make hundreds of such choices over the course of our lifetime. This prioritizing is part of the fabric of our character, the stuff of which our
character is made. It also determines to a great extent the nature of
a family, a culture, a nation, and a society.

We like to think that choosing one value over another is a
careful, deliberative process of *reasoning* or *rationality*. This may be
evidenced by our being able to explain the system by which we
choose and prioritize our values. From a strictly intellectual frame
of reference, this makes good sense, and when we are studying
philosophy, this is fine. But what happens when we are presented
with ethical dilemmas at times when our reasoning processes are
"down" or lethargic?

Suppose, for example, that after a hard day's work, you are
relaxing in front of the television. There, a Clint Eastwood movie
is dramatizing scenarios in which violent vengeance is prioritized
over justice, mercy, and compassion. After two hours of receiving
this repeated message, are you still rationally sorting out your
values?

To what extent do you adopt or give credence to such value
prioritizing, which was likely created for purposes much different
from helping define the fabric of your character?

Or suppose that you listen regularly to a "Top 40" rock radio
station, where you hear the latest hit repeated two or three times

each shift. This *redundancy* burns the song into your brain, perhaps unconsciously, until its lyrics have become part of your own personal truths. Educators know that the pedagogical device of repetition or rote learning is an integral part of how we acquire and hold information. (As the Queen informs Alice in Lewis Carroll's *Alice in Wonderland,* "What I tell you three times is true.")

From a strictly rational standpoint, we may never accept the values contained in the Clint Eastwood movie or the "Top 40" hit. But the values in such mass-mediated messages are usually not presented to us in settings of rationality. While we may implicitly understand this distinction, we often do not construct our reality in a manner that we can deal with it.

Here I readily admit that my own selection of rationally accepted messages over emotionally imposed ones is a *value prioritizing,* an ethical judgment on my part. This kind of ethics might be considered *individualistic ethics,* but it is a basic assumption of education that we should try to understand rationally the nature of our environment. Our communications environment is part of that environment, and the mass media furnish many messages in it. Thus, in this book we base value judgments on *rational* considerations in information processing.

Concerns about the settings in which we absorb mass media and their messages have brought about several contemporary events worth noting:

- The number of commercials people watch, the number of hours they spend watching television generally, and the often violent content of television programs have given rise to the assumption that certain kinds of effects may result from this exposure.
- Research on communications, specifically what are called uses and gratification studies, has looked at how media consumption affects behavior.
- Visible shifts in TV program content, in language in movies that filters into television and radio, and in the more recent explicitness of music lyrics and messages on records all have called new attention to the sets of values we hold as a society.
- In communications studies curricula at the college and university level, all these events have brought renewed attention of age-old concepts of ethics, values, morality, philosophy and decision making.

These events in turn raise some provocative questions:

- How much tolerance is there in a diverse, pluralistic society?
- If the media and their contents do not furnish options from which we can make satisfactory choices, where are our alternatives?
- What subset of our culture sets the values that the media reflect? Are the news judgments made by a local TV reporter "good" or "proper"? Who writes the made-for-TV movies we see on the tube, anyway?
- What are the standards or value systems the media should choose, and more important, who decides what they will be?

SOCIAL VALUES

To the extent that many individuals choose similar values, there is a kind of social cohesion—a commonality, or culture. These values are *social* in nature. When most members of a society or culture agree that a value is primary, they may go so far as to design a civil *law*—an agreed-upon norm for social conduct—to see that that value continues to be upheld.

Some social values may be considered of primary importance. The social value that human life has primacy, for example, is considered so important that laws have been made to protect human life and penalize anyone who takes it. The penalty for murder or homicide may be life imprisonment or even death.

Other social values may be less important but may nevertheless be reflected in laws, with penalties as consequences of violation. For example, traffic laws are designed to protect us from each other on the road. A street intersection may have stop signs or red lights to organize traffic flowing in various directions. A motorist who does not stop at the signs may be cited for violating a traffic law, even if there was no danger of collision with another vehicle.

Social values reflected in laws may conflict with an individual's personal values. Military conscription or draft laws may violate one's pacifist values based on one's religion. Or the social custom of saluting the flag may violate one's religious value that true veneration of and loyalty to God forbid such a gesture.

Widespread disagreement over values displayed in the media could result in a healthy, diverse, pluralistic society, or it could result in anarchy if the values that conflict are more fundamental and political.

When a group within society creates and agrees upon a set of guidelines for those within that group, that group norm becomes *codified*. Broadly, those codified norms are *laws*. Codified norms also are found in smaller organizations within society. Codes of a narrower scope may become *professional standards* or *professional codes*. Specific professionally oriented codes may be formalized into *codes of ethics*. An attorney has a special understanding of confidentiality with his or her client, according to a legal ethical code. The Hippocratic oath that a physician takes, swearing to preserve and prolong human life, is part of a medical code of ethics. An ethical business executive will deal honestly with clients. An ethical broadcast journalist does not "stage" or "recreate" news events, at least not without explicit acknowledgment of such. All of these are examples of *professional ethics*, or manifestations of the professionally agreed-upon norm known as a *professional code*.

Thus we move from individual values to more general principles that may be structured as laws or codes. In this evolution from values to principles to codes to ethics, let us stop to consider again the basic building blocks of values. What kinds of values are there? What are some basic examples?

Sociologist Milton Rokeach has identified some basic instrumental values and some terminal values. *Instrumental values* are those used as a means to accomplish an end—a way of getting there, to achieving a goal. *Terminal values* are the ends—where we hope to arrive, the most important goals of our activities.

Rokeach identifies 18 of the most common (as determined by survey) of each of these kinds of values in American society. They are listed here in a form that allows you to assess the priority or relative importance of each. You may rank them in order of their individual importance: 1 = the most important to 18 = the least important. How you rank them constitutes your own value set.

A class in a school or the employees of a television station may do this ranking collectively. This gives the group a sense of what values they collectively hold as most important.

Remember, right or wrong answers reside in the individual responder; there is no objective "right" answer, as there would be with a math problem. This is simply a personal prioritizing.

Instrumental Value	*Ranking*
Ambition (hard work, aspiration)	_____
Broadmindedness (open-mindedness)	_____
Capability (competence, effectiveness)	_____
Cheerfulness (lightheartedness, joyfulness)	_____
Cleanliness (neatness, tidiness)	_____
Courage (willingness to stand up for a belief)	_____
Forgiveness (willingness to pardon others)	_____
Helpfulness (willingness to work for others' welfare)	_____
Honesty (sincerity, truthfulness)	_____
Imagination (daringness, creativity)	_____
Independence (self-reliance, self-sufficiency)	_____
Intellect (intelligence, reflectiveness)	_____
Logicality (consistency, rationality)	_____
Love (affection, tenderness)	_____
Obedience (dutifulness, respect)	_____
Politeness (courtesy, well-manneredness)	_____
Responsibility (dependability, reliability)	_____
Self-control (restraint, self-discipline)	_____

Terminal Value	*Ranking*
Beauty (in nature and the arts)	_____
Comfort (prosperous life)	_____
Equality (brotherhood, equal opportunity)	_____
Excitement (stimulating, active life)	_____
Family security (safety of loved ones)	_____
Freedom (independence, free choice)	_____
Happiness (contentedness)	_____
Inner harmony (freedom from inner conflict)	_____
Mature love (sexual and spiritual intimacy)	_____
National security (safety from attack)	_____

Peace (a world free of war and conflict)   ————

Pleasure (enjoyment, leisure)   ————

Salvation (saved, eternal life)   ————

Self-respect (self-esteem)   ————

Sense of accomplishment (lasting contribution)   ————

Social recognition (respect, admiration)   ————

True friendship (close companionship)   ————

Wisdom (a mature understanding of life)   ————

Understandably, the prioritizing of these values will differ from individual to individual and from group to group. Each individual may have his or her own *set of values*. Such combinations of values constitute *individualistic ethics*. A person's unique prioritizing may generate criticism from other individuals or groups. This criticism or dissonance is what allows the creation and discussion of the dilemmas presented in the case studies.

There is always the temptation to impose one's own value judgments on another individual or group. Indeed, the very act of spotting what might seem a likely case study for discussion involves, itself, a value judgment as to whether this is an issue of ethics.

In a recent discussion of the propriety of airing 2-Live Crew's album *As Nasty as They Wanna Be*, an ethics class noted that the album uses the "f-word" 226 times and other profane words scores of times, to which one student asked, "So what's your point?"

Just presenting information, perhaps as objectively as possible, might be considered *descriptive ethics*. Presenting the information, for example, that senior-level media ethics students in a survey gave the highest priority to the value of "honesty" among the instrumental values in the above list and "freedom" among the terminal values only describes what is. Interpreting or comparing such survey results and asserting some kind of social standard against which to compare them would become *normative ethics*. Such evaluation takes into account the values behind the issue held by a group or a society. The *norm* is the average, the general rule, the recognized standard, although its priorities are not without challenges.

THE CHANGES IN NORMATIVE ETHICS

Value norms change, some very fast, others so slowly that they seem not to change at all. As various groups come to influence social values, the traditional values may be altered or change altogether. Fictional depictions of adulterous sexual liaisons in literature and motion pictures were once taboo. Now such themes are treated with somewhat more tolerance, if not acceptance. An older generation may remember that "indecent" language was never heard over the radio or in movies. Federal statutes forbid use of obscene or indecent language in broadcasting, reflecting previous norms of society. In the 1939 motion picture *Gone with the Wind,* when Scarlett O'Hara asks Rhett Butler what will become of her, he replies, "Frankly, my dear, I don't give a damn!" The use of the "d-word" was then thought to be scandalous. The changes in public language that have since occurred are obvious.

The changes in *social norms* involving language have come to be reflected in the media. Several colorful case studies that reflect these will be discussed in detail later in this book. Generally, the confrontation between traditional values of the past and those of the cutting edge of the future presents the structure for many of the case studies found here.

The following terms are critical in understanding the concepts in ethics. They have been defined or discussed in Chapter 1, and are listed here for the reader's convenience. Subsequent chapters will not contain lists of such orienting language.

List of Terms

aesthetics	normative ethics
codified norms	professional codes
descriptive ethics	reasoning, rationality
epistemology	redundancy in shaping values
ethics	social values
individualistic ethics	value prioritizing
instrumental values	value system
law	value set
norm	value

NOTES

1. KFKB Broadcasting Association, Inc. *v.* FRC, 47 F (2d) 670 at 671 (1931).
2. For a detailed discussion of professional codes of ethics, see Chapter 4.
3. *Co-op advertising* refers to advertising where a national advertiser, such as Budweiser beer, and a local beer distributor for that brand name both pay for the local advertisement.

2

Historical Perspectives

Should broadcast station licensees be allowed free rein to air whatever they desire? Should there be restraints? If so, where do they come from? Who should restrain? Where and how does one draw the line?

THE CASE OF REVEREND DR. SHULER

In the early days of radio, when the Federal Radio Commission (FRC) was establishing itself as a regulatory body, a case arose in which the FRC decided to revoke a license. The 1932 case pitted one Reverend Dr. Shuler, who operated KGEF in Los Angeles in behalf of the Trinity Methodist Church, South, against a number of local residents who felt that the reverend was operating a confidence racket with the station. In his broadcasts, Shuler would threaten personal attacks.

> On one occasion he announced over the radio that he had certain damaging information against a prominent unnamed man which, unless a contribution (presumably to the church) of a hundred dollars was forthcoming, he would disclose. As a result, he received contributions from several persons. He freely spoke of "pimps" and prostitutes. He alluded slightingly to the Jews as a race, and made frequent and bitter attacks on the Roman Catholic religion and its relations to government.[1]

Was Shuler's conduct improper? He might have argued that what he was doing was attempting to rid society of some personal and social evils. He did not force anyone to contribute to the church; it was their conscience that prompted their "contributions." He had his right to his opinions about other classes and religions in society, did he not? Wasn't his First Amendment right of free speech being taken away by a government body whose mission was to regulate only frequencies and technical standards?

The residents who were fighting Shuler felt that he was using the "public's airwaves" to obstruct the orderly administration of justice. Since the FRC, as a government body, was acting in behalf of the people to administer the best use of radio's "ether" (that is, use of frequency allocation in electromagnetic radiation), it had the right to revoke a license. As it happened, that was the way the federal district court decided this case.

Both parties in this case felt that the values they held were more important than those of their opponent. Such *value conflicts* are the kinds of situations of which ethics debates and law cases are made.

Upon what values, however, has the broadcast industry been established?

Shortly after radio broadcasting caught on as a means of public communication, many people and organizations obtained transmitters and started their own "stations." There were ministers who were impressed with the size of the congregation that radio could muster. There were educational institutions that thought that radio could transform every living room in the United States into a classroom. There were department stores and manufacturers eager to use radio to create markets. All entered the "ether." By the mid-1920s, the airwaves had become chaotic. Everyone was trying to shoulder his or her way into the radio spectrum.

THE CASE OF EVANGELIST AIMEE SEMPLE MCPHERSON

One colorful example of this was the popular radio evangelist Aimee Semple McPherson. From her temple in Los Angeles, she operated a radio station that had a tendency to wander over the dial, interfering with a number of other stations. Although there had been some attempt to assign frequencies by this time (1922), McPherson paid little attention to such a secular demand.

After one government order to her to stay within the recommended range, the evangelist responded to then–Secretary of Commerce Herbert Hoover, "Please order your minions of Satan to leave my station alone. You cannot expect the almighty to abide by your wavelength nonsense. When I offer my prayers to him, I must fit into his wave reception. Open this station at once."[2] When the evangelist finally agreed to hire a competent engineer, the station was allowed to stay on the air.

THE ORIGINAL RATIONALE FOR GOVERNMENT REGULATION

This elbowing for room on the limited spectrum of radio frequencies led to more battles over authority, frequency, and power. Finally, the resulting chaos demonstrated the need for congressional legislation, first passing the Radio Act of 1927, then the Communications Act of 1934. The latter act authorized that a Federal Communications Commission (FCC) be set up to administer the allocation of the spectrum frequencies. The original premise seemed to be that the FCC would serve as a "traffic cop," ensuring that one signal did not interfere with another.

The subsequent system was set up on two premises: (1) the *scarcity of frequencies,* hence the need for the FCC to decide which bidders would be allowed to actually operate a station, and (2) the *presumption of power.* Already radio was persuading people to buy, learn, and allow their tastes in entertainment to be shaped. The FCC was to ensure that consumers were protected against unscrupulous hucksterism on the public airwaves. The FCC was thus a quasi-judicial agency that had not only rule-making power but the power to adjudicate disputes among parties vying for station licenses.

In a sense, the creation of the FCC reflected concern about the possibility of broadcasting that was not in the best interests of the public or the government. To make their judgments, commissioners drew on a set of value judgments. Whose values should radio broadcasting reflect—those of station licensees? Consumers and listeners? Government bureaucrats? Lobbyists? The commissioners' own personal values? It is probably safe to say that in actuality FCC judgments reflected all these values.

It was not long before the Commission's jurisdiction was extended from the "traffic cop" function among stations to checking the substantive content of programming itself. To some people, that jurisdiction seemed to conflict with First Amendment guarantees against government intrusion on the right of free speech. Eventually, in 1946, the FCC issued its "Blue Book," officially titled *Public Service Responsibilities of Broadcast Licensees.* Everything from "non-entertainment program requirements" to the logging of all programs by type subsequently became a near-obsession of the Commission. This effort was the Commission's way of enforcing its mandate to ensure that the public's airwaves were used in the "public interest, convenience and necessity."

Over time, some of the values of the FCC enforcers had changed, and there were now different expectations from this promising young medium of radio as well. What were some of the elements that brought about these changes?

The *broadcast industry* itself was, of course, an influence. The values it set forth both influenced and reflected the FCC and subsequent regulation. Some of the language that expresses the values that helped shape radio and eventually broadcasting generally is presented in the 1929 Code of Good Practice of Radio Broadcasting:

> Recognizing that the radio audience includes persons of all ages and all types of political, social and religious belief, every broadcast will endeavor to prevent the broadcasting of any matter which would commonly be regarded as offensive.

The values evident in this early code are *responsibility, tolerance,* and *respect for others' values.*

VALUE JUXTAPOSITION: COMPARING AND ANALYZING VALUES

Hopefully, the values identified in the 1929 code are obvious to the reader, since for many of the case studies in this book, the reader will be asked to identify values in this way in order to develop a full understanding of basic values. Identification of values alone, however, may not help much with interpretation or analysis. To compare one's set of values with another's is revealing, and identifying the values of one era and comparing them with those of contemporary times divulges information about history and our own society.

This method might be termed *value juxtaposition*. It can be a valuable tool in ethical analysis as well as in historical-descriptive analysis.

Using the two historical anecdotes of the Reverend Dr. Shuler and Aimee Semple McPherson, one could examine the premise that radio broadcasting in the 1920s followed to some extent the motto of U.S. business at that time: "Let the buyer [listener] beware." In other words, the interests of the broadcast licensee took primacy over those of the listener, which had a lower priority. When government began to intervene in this arrangement through the FCC, it was criticized for upsetting a system, even though on the surface there seemed to be justification for the government to do so.

Today, the right of government to regulate and intervene in both broadcasting and business generally seems commonplace and unquestioned to many. Perhaps the "consumer rights" movement has made such inroads that we now expect the values of consumer protection to dominate in our society, even at the risk of government intervention. The recent social history of this movement and its effect on broadcasting could be analyzed by comparing the social milieu of the 1930s with that of today, by the method of value juxtaposition.

A value juxtaposition analysis could also be made of Aimee Semple McPherson's apparent devotion to worship via radio in the 1920s with today's ideas about praying over radio. To many people in our time, such devotion seems fanatical and even amusing. In the two generations since her era, we know, radio has produced many claims, some of them fraudulent. By now, we have learned to be skeptical.

THE VALUES OF BROADCASTING'S EARLY PROMISE

Excitement over broadcasting's potential spread quickly. Colleges and universities were sure that instead of students coming to a campus and sitting in classrooms with four sterile walls and a chalkboard to listen to lectures, they could stay at home, out on the farm, or wherever, and listen to the same lectures. Extension agents were to coordinate this new effort. Certainly, radio could revolutionize higher education!

One experiment in this form of education occurred at Washington State College (now Washington State University), a land grant institution. There, microphone experiments developed by Homer Dana, a professor of electrical engineering, were merged with the tasks of the land-grant extension agents. The result was the licensing in 1922 of KRFA radio, which aired radio lectures on agronomy and crop rotation along with a whole host of other subjects.

Even for those not formally enrolled in an educational institution, the instructional potential was exciting! They greeted with enthusiasm radio's ability to bring them the events of the world, new horizons in sciences, and the refinement of the fine arts. One of the first publicly broadcast events was the 1920 Harding-Cox election returns on KDKA, in Pittsburgh. However, as the novelty of radio wore off, radio lectures began to be ignored.

At about this time, merchants were discovering that radio provided them with a captive audience for their sales pitches. But in order to gain the largest possible audience, programs had to be of wide interest—entertainment programs, popular artists singing and playing the songs of the day—not the less popular radio lectures. Later, there were popular melodramas. High culture was evolving into *popular culture*. The public's taste for the programming on radio had evolved from excitement over its potential to an accustomed convention.

Perhaps only those with a sense of that 1920s excitement are in a position today to compare the early values with later ones. One such juxtaposition was made by Lee de Forest, the developer of the key component of radio, the audion tube, and the "Father of Radio":

> Throughout my long career I have lost no opportunity to cry out in earnest protest against the crass commercialism, the etheric vandalism of the vulgar hucksters, agencies, advertisers, station owners—all who, lacking awareness of their grand opportunities and moral responsibilities to make of radio an uplifting influence, continue to enslave and sell for quick cash the grandest medium which has yet been given to man to help upward his struggling spirit.[3]

Later, de Forest told broadcasters: "You have debased my child. . . . You have made him a laughingstock of intelligence . . . a stench in the nostrils of the gods of the ionosphere."[4]

Obviously, the values reflected by de Forest's remarks seem extreme when compared with those of today's typical observer of broadcasting. It may be true, however, that a lack of understanding of the original mission of broadcasting creates an illusion of extremism. Some scholars have indicated that before we dismiss de Forest's rhetoric as fanatical, we need to examine the value systems of early broadcasting. The closer we look at de Forest's position, the more we may come to understand why he articulated it.

FACTORS THAT CHANGED BROADCASTING'S ORIGINAL VALUES

Why did radio become something other than what Lee de Forest expected it would become? Several factors came into the mix.

Rivalry with the Press

Radio almost did not become a news medium at all. One of the driving factors for newspaper journalists of the day was to "scoop," to be first with a story. It was part of the definition of good journalism to have the story before the competition got it. Since radio could deliver a story almost instantly—literally, at the speed of sound as it was transmitted—it would always be able to scoop its news rival, the newspaper. The press of the day simply considered radio a threat.

By 1933, newspapers had pressured the news wire services (which were an integral part of both the radio and newspaper news industries) to cut off service to radio stations. The press also lobbied Congress to pass stronger restrictions on direct news broadcasting over radio. (This may seem incredible in light of journalists' supposed dedication to the First Amendment, which prohibits government intervention in freedom of the press.)

In 1934 the government set up the Press Radio Bureau to ensure that radio stations were restricted to broadcasting only ten minutes of news a day. Radio news reports could not be commercially sponsored, and they could be aired only *after* that news had appeared in newspapers. Senator Clarence C. Dill of Washington, who had helped draft the Communications Act of 1934, called these policies "tyrannical and indefensible," and he criticized not only the hypocritical press but the radio networks for having "surrendered radio's birthright."[5]

Eventually, in 1940, the policies were changed, and radio worked to overcome its inferiority complex about its journalistic role. Soon, figures came on the scene—Edward R. Murrow, H. V. Kaltenborn, and others—who legitimized radio as a news medium. World War II created a great appetite in the American public to hear—instantly—what was happening in other parts of the world.

News became popular—and salable. Merchants who longed for large-market exposure for their advertisements were willing to pay handsome sums to have their commercials accompany the radio news.

News soon became "commercial"—worthy of popular appeal and a necessary element of radio's obligation to serve its public. Without objection, the FCC required stations to carry at least a few minutes daily of "non entertainment" programming—news.

Some observers in government, however, felt that the new-found success of radio in the area of news was based too much on opportunism. In 1946, when the FCC issued its Blue Book, it indicated that when a station's license came up for renewal, the Commission would look at how responsibly the station was broadcasting "sustaining" programs (that is, programs inappropriate for commercial sponsorship), *local live* programs, and discussions of public issues. In order to do this properly, the Commission required a station to survey its market or community to determine the most pressing issues on which it could shed light through its news and public affairs programs. This requirement became known as *ascertainment of community needs.*

Radio news had gone from being government-prohibited to being government-required—a striking shift in societal values about radio.

Eventually, living up to the FCC standards articulated in the Blue Book became a bureaucratic burden, full of dangerous pitfalls for even the most cautious of broadcasters. During the Reagan administration, government bureaucracy that conflicted with enterprise was reduced. Requirements that radio stations ascertain community needs or even carry news programming at all were largely done away with. Today one may listen variously to a station that has no news whatsoever, or one that has a sprinkling of news each hour, or one that is *all* news.

In summary, the radio as a journalistic medium has edged from being a kind of *informational-educative* source of news to serving commercial and popular interests. One may logically argue that the shift was necessary in order to keep broadcasting economically healthy, but the point here is that values concerning the role of radio in news have shifted.

Broadcasting in a Free Enterprise Economy

At the time when radio broadcasting emerged, the United States had discovered that the path to success was paved not only with hard work but with an ability to compete successfully in the economic marketplace and to invest in profit-making enterprises. It took much of the nineteenth century to prove Adam Smith's theories that the free pursuit of individual enterprise brings industry and overall good to society. Even the best of ideas, the best of inventions, and the noblest of intentions were doomed to failure if there was no economic support to carry them on.

One could respond to Lee de Forest's criticism by noting that if radio did not have a way of making money (advertising being the best-proved formula for doing that), it would fail, even if it had the very highest of aspirations.

Very early in the days of radio, it was thought that the medium could be supported economically through sales of radio receiving sets themselves. Manufacturers were among the first station licensees to attempt to drive the market for radio purchases. But what would happen when the market became saturated and most households had receivers? Could sales of radios always provide enough financial backing to support hours of programming each day? One might note that foreign radio broadcasting systems that have tried other means of economic support, such as government underwriting, have since moved to the free-enterprise, capitalistic system that started very early in the United States.[6]

All values that have to do with being practical, being successful, and being able to attain goals would seem to support this economic underpinning. "Commercialism," as distasteful as it may seem to some, is simply a necessary function of how things work in broadcasting or any other enterprise in our economic system.

The issue of the profit incentive is considered here for two important reasons. First, it demonstrates how the economics of broadcasting changed some of the developers' original intentions. And second, in the conflicts presented in the case studies in this book, the most common value on one side is that of the *profit incentive*. Making money in itself is not necessarily a "bad" thing, but in competition with other means, it can become a "vice." It is wise to remember when considering these case studies just what else goes along with the profit incentive as a motivation.

The Acceptance of Popular Culture

While early expectations of radio were that it would make broadly accessible information, education, and the *high arts*, listeners soon grew weary of such fare. Operatic arias were replaced by popular songs, often played by musical groups in the studios themselves. While some room seemed to remain for "classical" music and drama, listeners seemed to respond more to contemporary music and melodrama.

In the 1930s much of vaudeville moved from the stage to the radio studio. Radio soap operas, mysteries, comedies, light music, and similar programming began to define what radio really was. As a matter of fact, such programming began to define the popular arts in America.

From the singing, dancing, and slapstick comedy routines of vaudeville came the program *Amos 'n' Andy,* in which two white performers used a number of Black dialects to achieve comedy characters. In the context of its time, it captured some of the stereotypes of Black America, unflattering as they seem today. Examining the program and comparing its values with those of today by the use of value juxtaposition, the program would probably appear to be racist, even though the show was as popular and accepted by Blacks then as by anyone else.

How popular was it? Traffic would stop when the program came on, and the business of early evening in major cities would subside. Movies would be halted at seven in the evening so that listeners could catch the next 15-minute episode and the characters' antics. Remember, this was during the 1930s depression, and the program portrayed what most people were experiencing—hard times, or poverty.

The radio networks were becoming stronger and could wrest stars away from motion pictures. In the 1940s radio entered its "Golden Era," when programs featured famous stars: Fred Allen, Ed Wynn, Al Jolson, Groucho Marx, Jack Benny, Bing Crosby, Red Skelton, George Burns and Gracie Allen, Edgar Bergen and Charlie McCarthy, and so on. No longer was it possible for radio to return to a simple educational and informational function. It was now at the forefront of popular culture, listened to by millions of Americans every week—listeners who expected to be *entertained*.

Responsiveness Through Community Ascertainment

Originally, when a radio station was given its license, it promised to exercise responsibility for the "public's airwaves" by airing programming that would be for the best good of the public—the "public interest, convenience and necessity." Eventually, as we have seen, the FCC mandated or required that stations go out into the community and survey or interview community leaders—business leaders, civic leaders, ministers, and others—to ascertain what the needs of the community were. The radio station owners would presumably use this information to develop news and public affairs programming. The ascertainment requirement became an important bureaucratic regulation.

Few would argue with its intent. If use of the public airwaves entailed responsibility, knowing what was important in the community seemed key to that responsibility.

DEREGULATION AND THE VALUE OF "TRUST"

But as the government bureaucracy became more streamlined during the 1980s, many people began to ask themselves: "Can't this responsibility be demonstrated without its being shoved down broadcasters' throats? What if *trust* were the key factor, rather than community ascertainment, and broadcasters were allowed to demonstrate on their own how they reflected community needs and concerns? Furthermore, what if its success were measured in terms of audience response—the number of listeners and viewers who were really interested in the issues aired? Wouldn't that, after all, be the best measure in a 'free marketplace economy'?"

This position of *trust* is what governs broadcast regulation today. It has replaced values of *mistrust* and government intervention on the public's behalf. There are many people who think that such deregulation is not in the public's best interest—that the government must be ever vigilant against unscrupulous persons or businesses that will try to take advantage and make money off of a *public resource*, the broadcast spectrum.

What is your own evaluation?

Examine the values involved on both sides: the idea of *government regulation*, exemplified by mandated ascertainment of community needs, versus the idea of *deregulation*, exemplified by trust. Like the other issues examined here, this one comes down to a matter of prioritizing one set of values over another. Do you agree with the way deregulation has evolved? Or do you see any justification for the more traditional perspective of government as watchdog?

Move Over, Education

In 1923, 12 percent of all radio stations were licensed to educational institutions. They operated on a noncommercial basis as a deliberate structural choice. Eventually, as broadcasting from noneducational institutions was becoming commercial, "educational" broadcasting tried to steer away from advertising and commercial support. Many educational stations viewed commercial support as compromising or distasteful. Some of the educational stations gave up their frequencies to licensees, and they ended up becoming commercial anyway. Today, there are only a handful of noncommercial AM radio stations in existence.

Had an injustice been committed when frequencies were allocated for educational purposes, when educational radio had no clear potential for growth through monetary profits? Perhaps it was a negative answer to this question that prompted the FCC in 1945 to set aside 20 of the 100 FM channels for noncommercial broadcasting. At this time, the move didn't seem like a big deal to commercial broadcasters, since the audience for the new medium of FM radio was still limited; hardly anyone even had an FM receiver.

More recently, however, now that FM radio has become extremely valuable commercial property, some broadcasting entrepreneurs have raised a clamor to acquire the channels that were set aside for noncommercial purposes.

What do you think about it? Is the profit incentive and the proven money-making ability of FM broadcasting a higher priority than educational functions? After all, the commercial media also inform, instruct, and educate. To what extent do we still hold to that early value of broadcasting as an educational tool? Is radio being "debased," as Lee de Forest said, by its commercialism? Or is its "commercialism" the very basis of healthy growth that would not otherwise be possible? Just where is there room for educational functions? Can we arrive at a compromise to allow some educational broadcasting and still allow for plenty of business opportunity in the industry? Some observers believe that the current setup, in which some channels are set aside for noncommercial use, is an optimal compromise, one that seems to accommodate values on both sides.

Modeled after this "set-aside" idea, television from its inception has had noncommercial advocates who have pushed for classifying some TV channels as noncommercial. The idea was promoted at the time when the FCC was shaping allocations for television—during the _TV freeze_ (no granting of more TV licenses between 1948 and 1952), when the FCC decided on standards of color and on the frequencies from the UHF band, channels 14 to 86. In 1952 "educational TV" ended up with over 200 channel allocations nationwide.

In 1967, Congress passed the Public Broadcasting Act, which gave government funding to what was once called "educational" broadcasting but, because of the stigmas attached to educational functions, was now called "public broadcasting."

Today, educational radio and television share the same dilemma: how to hold on to interesting (usually expensive) programs, attract an audience, and still have enough money for the payroll. Government funds just don't seem to go far enough. So supplemental help has come to local public stations in the form of _commercial underwriting,_ in which a business or organization gives a noncommercial station financial support, which the station then acknowledges along with a one-line promotion of that organization.

Is commercial underwriting a "sellout" for public broadcasting? A purist might consider the values of *independence* from any commercial interests whatsoever to be primary. Other, more compromising observers might consider commercial underwriting as the best possible compromise: financial support that is acknowledged but without any "hype and hucksterism," as might be found in commercial advertising.

SOME PHILOSOPHIES FROM WHICH VALUE JUDGMENTS COME

The Golden Mean

In some philosophical approaches these two compromises—noncommercial channel allocations and commercial underwriting—might be regarded as ideal. Seeking the best possible position between two opposing or clashing values, which ethicists call the *golden mean,* was expressed centuries ago by Aristotle:

> For the man who flies from and fears everything and does not stand his ground against anything becomes a coward, and the man who fears nothing at all but goes to meet every danger becomes rash; and similarly the man who indulges in every pleasure and abstains from none becomes self-indulgent, while the man who shuns every pleasure, as boors do, becomes in a way insensible; temperance and courage, then, are destroyed by excess and defect, and preserved by the mean.[7]

Thus, virtue is the appropriate location between two extremes. Aristotle admitted, however, to some values or virtues that did not lend themselves to compromise:

> But not every action nor every passion admits of a mean; for some have names that already imply badness, e.g., spite, shamelessness, envy, and in the case of actions adultery, theft, murder . . . simply to do any of them is to go wrong.[8]

The Categorical Imperative

This idea of holding uncompromisingly to a virtue is more widely associated with the German philosopher Immanuel Kant and is known as the *categorical imperative:*

There is . . . only a single categorical imperative and it is this: Act only on that maxim through which you can at the same time will that it should become a universal law.[9]

In other words, there is virtue in holding to what you see as an important truth.

The Principle of Utility

Still another philosophical approach to ethics may dominate in the value judgments one is making: basing them on their practicality or workability. Philosopher John Stuart Mill wrote of this *principle of utility*.

The creed which accepts as the foundation of morals Utility, or the Greatest Happiness Principle, holds that actions are right in proportion as they tend to promote happiness, wrong as they tend to produce the reverse of happiness.[10]

As a person makes decisions concerning ethics, he or she draws on a personal set of values. Which values are given priority and brought into play may depend on which philosophy one can embrace.

Any or all three of these philosophies may dominate a decision-making process in the situations, case studies, and historical happenings discussed in this book. There are, of course, more philosophies than the three identified here, and some of them will be introduced in later chapters.

NOTES

1. Trinity Methodist Church, South *v.* FRC, 62 F. (2d) 850 at 852 (1932).
2. Herbert Hoover, *Memoirs,* vol. 2 (New York: Macmillan, 1952): 142.
3. Lee de Forest, *Father of Radio* (Chicago: Wilcox and Follett Co., 1950): 442–43.
4. Lee de Forest, address to the National Association of Broadcasters, quoted in his obituary in *Time* (July 7, 1961), p. 67.
5. Clarence C. Dill, "Radio and the Press: A Contrary View," *Annals of the American Academy of Political and Social Science* 177 (Jan. 1935): 170–75.
6. Most European countries' radio broadcasting systems were government operated and government funded, usually by a tax on radio sets. These

systems lasted until the 1960s and 1970s, when they were replaced with the advertising-based system familiar in the United States.

7. Aristotle, *Nichomachean Ethics* (1104a), bk. 2, chap. 2, 11. 20–25.
8. Aristotle, *Nichomachean Ethics* (1107b), bk. 2, chap. 6, 11. 10–18.
9. Immanuel Kant, *The Metaphysic of Morals* (1797), chap. 11.
10. John Stuart Mill, *Utilitarianism* (1861), chap. 2.

3

Making Value Decisions About Television Use

Much of the literature developed in the field of broadcasting ethics concerns the subject of news. Much of this literature focuses on the decision-making processes of television journalists and news personnel. Later in this book, we will also discuss that part of the process of value prioritizing.

In this chapter, however, our focus is on the recipients of broadcasting. It should be remembered that although news directors make news judgments and although program creators, producers, and directors make program judgments, the final say in what stays on television or radio rests with the viewers or listeners. This is the "law" of popular culture in our current system: The number of viewers and listeners determines what goes or stays on the air. A lack of broad appeal may well mean the demise of a program.

Marshall McLuhan called attention to the need to focus on the recipients of media messages, their setting, and the medium's use when he indicated that it was not so much a medium's content that is the message but "the medium is the message." How we observe a medium reveals the real impact.[1]

Note this situation:

Case Study 3.1: A Heavy-Viewing Family

Even before the children were born, a constant blue-white light emanated from the Davis family home. Television had been an important part of Ed and Ila Davis's lives ever since they could remember. As a girl, Ila had been a member of the Mickey Mouse Club. Ed had once visited the Rex Ranger Show for his birthday and had actually seen Mr. Ranger.

Except for television, the Davises' day-to-day life was relatively boring. There was something absolutely compelling about this source of laughter and tears, this constant companion, this window on the world. Ed dreamed of being an emcee on a TV quiz show. Ila knew thoroughly all the characters in five soap operas that came on every day—even though the shows were all on at the same time. Flipping channels using the remote control ("grazing") and recording programs on one channel while watching another made that possible. TV brought the Davises glamour, excitement and romance.

Now Ed and Ila are both grown and have two children of their own.

Their son, Billy, is nine years old. He watches television about 50 hours a week: before school for an hour, after school for two hours, and during the evenings for three hours. On Saturdays and Sundays, he watches about ten hours each day. During the summer he has many ten-hour TV days. His total viewing time is more than double the number of hours he spends in school. It exceeds every other waking activity, including communication with other people, most notably his parents.

Not only is Billy a heavy viewer of television, he is physically heavy for his age. The two are related: Because he's busy watching TV, he does not participate much in sports or outdoor activities. When he tries, his peers make fun of his slowness and clumsiness—he has not yet developed any athletic abilities. This situation deepens Billy's indifference to doing things with his friends. He has become *asocial*, in a sense.

Much of Billy's world revolves around the characters he sees on television: Ninja Turtles and G.I. Joe and a whole array of cartoon characters. He can also watch old reruns of 1960s TV programs, thanks to the convenience of cable channels. At issue here, however, is less Billy's involvement with particular TV characters than Billy himself—his physical development, his social skills, his maturation into an adult human being.

Billy's parents found that his trouble-making in his earlier years subsided when they urged him to simply sit down and watch television. Even though TV surely has made life much simpler for them, they now wonder if there is too much TV in their son's life.

Ed and Ila were not concerned at first. One of their neighbors, who'd had a heavy-viewing child in his own family, assured the Davises that Billy would outgrow it. Watching television, he said, is actually good for children—it brings them to see experiences they normally would not see. It helps make them wiser sooner than they would be with no TV. But Ila's mother, Grandma Martin, expressed concern that Billy could barely read and was having trouble generally in school. The nine-year-old hardly knew how to carry on a conversation. Watching television, she said, would only make Billy dumber and dumber.

Two years earlier, when the family's only TV set was in the shop for repairs, the Davises had experienced anxiety, irritability, aggression, and boredom. The children became objects of verbal abuse. When their TV "friend" came back, those symptoms disappeared.

Is television a tutor and learning aid for Davises? Or, in your assessment, is there anything "bad" in Billy's situation—are there negative values in his television viewing? Is TV a villain in his life that on a wider scale will mean his educational downfall?

If it is, what values would be embraced by denying Billy his television-watching schedule?

Some research suggests that TV is addictive, much like a drug. Marie Winn calls TV a "plug-in drug."[2] In order to test the idea of TV addiction, several researchers have studied families who tried to give up TV viewing. In the studies, family members reported nervousness, depression, and many of the other characteristics that are also symptomatic of drug addicts trying to withdraw.[3]

One possible, if extreme reaction to the perceived negative values of television-watching is to rid our lives of TV altogether. Such a strategy has been laid out by Jerry Mander in his book *Four Arguments for the Elimination of Television.*[4]

Is there room for an attitude toward heavy TV viewing and its effects, however, that is more moderate, friendlier, than total withdrawal? Such a perspective might be that a more moderate viewing schedule would somehow be "better" than either extreme. Then we must ask, "better" by what standard, by which values?

How is it that the extreme of *heavy viewing* removes the virtue of the gift of television?

Researchers have studied the subject and the "animal" of the heavy television-viewing schedule. They have found that people who watch TV heavily have the following characteristics:

- *Loneliness.* Those who lack much social interaction, have few friends, or are experiencing alienating factors in their lives are likely to turn to TV for companionship and escape.
- *Emotional difficulties.* Depression and anxiety make normal patterns of communication difficult, but TV requires no overt response from the viewer.
- *Youth.* Since social skills, experience, self-control, and education have not yet developed in young people, television is a congenial companion for them since it forgives all such immaturity.
- *Low income.* Playing golf, sailing, and attending an opera are expensive avocations. In fact, most activities, private or social, require money. But it is less expensive—and easier—simply to stay home and watch television.
- *Lack of education.* Often associated with a low income, a lack of education is also associated with a lack of language skills and a lack of knowledge about things that could occupy a person's leisure time. TV viewing requires no previous experience or education.
- *Availability of free time.* Persons who have little to do can usually pass the time in watching television. From children with no schedules, to adults who are not working (whether or not by choice), to retired persons, heavy viewing crosses all lifestyles.

TELEVISION AND LEISURE TIME

In our society it has long been thought that how we spend our free time shows who we really are. Perhaps we are among those who feel guilty about "wasting time." Traditionally, positive societal values have favored those who fill their leisure hours with productive activities—crafts, the arts, reading, even maintaining physical health by simply exerting oneself. Correspondingly, negative values have been associated with the imprudent use of time. Such people were considered lazy, unproductive, lacking in self-control, unimaginative, lacking in accomplishment, and the like.

As early as the twenty-fourth century B.C., a stated maxim was: "Do not lessen the time of following desire, for the wasting of time is an abomination to the spirit."[5] In ancient Greece, it was thought that those who had the good fortune of not having to work for a living would use the time to "school" their mind. Indeed, the Greek word for leisure is *schole,* the origin of our word *school.* The Romans added the ideas of physical fitness and applied knowledge, leading to an active, useful life.

Of course, ancient quotes give credence to the idea that there is some kind of wisdom that passes down through the ages—some kind of ageless truth. But in later centuries, the Church embraced the idea that "leisure is the father of all vices," an idea that came to be part of the Puritan work ethic. And to Ben Franklin is attributed the remark, "Dost thou love life? Then do not squander time; for that's the stuff life is made of."[6]

This idea has been passed down to twentieth-century thinkers who equate the unwise use of leisure time with the greatest waste in American life. Some have warned that people who have much leisure time left after work may pose a danger if they do not know how to guide their own behavior during that time. Can we really be trusted with the free time accorded us by the ingenious "labor-saving" devices of our age?

In the mid-1950s, when television watching had already gained its strong grip on American leisure habits, the Group for the Advancement of Psychiatry "expressed formal concern that leisure actually posed a 'significant danger' to many Americans."[7] Contemporary thinker and educator Robert Hutchins has warned, "More free time means more time to waste. The worker who used to have only a little free time in which to get drunk and beat his wife now has time to get drunk, beat his wife—and watch TV."[8]

Perhaps it was good fortune, then, that at about the time the work week began to shrink in the United States, television came along to fill the void. With its narcotizing effects, other commentators believe, television may help reduce an otherwise mischievous use of time. But then, could it not discourage ingenious and creative use of time as well?

In the late twentieth century, the most widespread leisure activity that Americans share in common is watching television. If magazines are an index of our interests and how we use our leisure time, then the fact that the most widely circulated magazine is *TV Guide* leads us to conclude that television is our dominant leisure activity. True, that magazine's dissemination of TV schedules might be an indication of discrete and highly selective viewing habits. Or it simply may reflect our obsession with television and its various aspects. Obviously, not all viewers are the heavy viewers discussed above. Perhaps most people watch television lightly or casually.

The question here is the association of positive or negative values with the use or abuse of leisure time. If watching television is the most popular leisure-time activity, then watching television itself, *regardless of what is watched,* must be the focus of any discussion of personal ethics associated with television. If spending time watching television is a kind of "time abuse," then is heavy viewing a gross abuse of time? On the other hand, is it meaningful to discuss content? Is watching a science program on public television of the same value as watching a forgettable sitcom or never-ending soap opera? In asking such questions, as well as answering them, we bring our value systems into play. It is both a social issue and an issue involving personal ethics. Since everyone has some kind of personal ethics or set of values, everyone is capable of reacting to the values seen on television.

In the minds of such observers our consumption of television continues even as we deride much of what it gives us. Columnist George Will has been quoted as saying, "Disparagement of television is second only to watching television as a national pastime." We live in a kind of schizophrenic world where we both shun and embrace, both laugh at and laugh with television. And all the while, we only dimly understand its consequences. Our cognitive senses are at rest, while our affective senses laugh at the good times that the bards of Hollywood bring us via the tube.

In his work aptly entitled *Amusing Ourselves to Death,* Neil Postman notes:

> Everything in our background has prepared us to know and resist a prison when the gates begin to close around us. . . . But what if there are no cries of anguish to be heard? Who is prepared to take arms against a sea of amusements? To whom do we complain, and when, and in what tone of voice, when serious discourse dissolves into giggles? What is the antidote to a culture's being drained by laughter? . . .
>
> [I]n the end [Aldous Huxley] was trying to tell us that what afflicted the people in *Brave New World* was not that they were laughing instead of thinking, but that they did not know what they were laughing about and why they had stopped thinking.[9]

If people's values and cognitive processes are formed early in life, and if television plays a major role in the life of most children, it is perhaps significant to examine the role of television in the child's formative learning processes.

THE SHAPING OF TELEVISION VIEWING HABITS IN CHILDHOOD

It has been established that the shaping of personal ethics by viewing television begins early in life. Media consumption patterns reveal that older people read newspapers with more dedication than do younger people. And conversely, younger people watch television more. In fact, the younger the age group, the heavier the general use of TV. Today, most of the U.S. population—those under 50—have grown up with television and probably have had only rare experiences of life without it. Like fish in water, it is difficult for people today to imagine existence without TV. This makes exploring and assessing values with and without TV, and values formed from TV, a great challenge.

Perhaps a good place to begin such an exploration is to examine the relationship between children and television. Much research has focused on children's television-watching habits. Even early in television's history, two important presumptions about children's TV-watching became clear. First, television is highly attractive to children, indeed compulsively so, especially to children between the ages of three and eight, the age when their important conceptual thinking is forming. Second, television profoundly affects many aspects of the behavior of children.

Case Study 3.2: The Restricted-Viewing Family

Scott and Connie Stuart are both well read. Scott is an engineer; he designs and sells his ideas in a manner that allows his family to live quite comfortably. His wife spends much of her time volunteering at the library and the hospital and generally doing community service. They both spend considerable time sitting before a television screen—each more than 40 hours a week. But the "TV screen" in their case is the monitor of a computer.

The Stuarts have a six-year-old son and a three-year-old daughter. Having read about the studies on the effects of television on young children, Scott and Connie have set strict rules about watching TV for their children. They keep the regular viewing set locked in a cabinet and pull it out regularly so that the children can watch *Sesame Street* or *Mister Rogers' Neighborhood*. On occasion, for a special happening such as a political speech or a *National Geographic Special*, the family gathers around and watches together; such events are carefully planned. Sometimes the Stuarts rent videotapes with children's adventure programs or other movies that they know to be suitable for their children to watch.

Whenever his parents pull the television out of the cabinet, six-year-old Tom is fascinated. He has discovered that his friends are not restricted in their TV-watching, and on one or two occasions, Tom has gone to their houses supposedly to play ball but actually to watch cartoon programs. Soon such clandestine viewing becomes frequent. After all, with all its colorful animation and action, TV is "fun" for Tom to watch. When his parents ask him what he does at his friends' homes, Tom has to cover up or outright lie. Soon he begins to feel guilty. For Tom, conventional television viewing has become a taboo experience, with negative values on either side of the taboo, depending on the person's point of view.

Is this "suppression" of television viewing developing positive traits in Tom and the sets of values that Connie and Scott intend? Despite their intentions, in other words, is such secret behavior bad? How should the Stuarts react if they discover Tom's secret TV-viewing? Should they punish him and try to control his activities outside home more strictly? Or should they allow more leniency in his TV-viewing at home? How do your answers reflect your own values? Where might you go for information that will shed more light on the subject? Note that the issue here is a combination of concern about extent of viewing *and* the content or substance of the programs seen.

The effect of television-watching on children is perhaps the single most researched subject in the social sciences today. A rich resource of literature in this area has been produced. As early as the 1970s, at the request of Congress, the U.S. Surgeon General compiled an extensive list of studies to determine TV's effects on children.[10] His recommendation indicated that television, especially televised violence, has a profound effect and that the television industry should be sensitive to that fact:

The overwhelming consensus and the unanimous Scientific Advisory Committee's report indicate that televised violence, indeed, does have an adverse effect on certain members of our society. . . . the causal relationship between televised violence and antisocial behavior is sufficient to warrant appropriate and immediate remedial action.[11]

Today, in the mind of anyone familiar with the extensive research, there is little doubt that television has a consequential impact on the mind, behavior, and values of young viewers.

Since television affects children so profoundly, many people have wondered whether perhaps TV can be manipulated to effect a positive influence on children. (Note that the word *positive* is value-laden. A more functional term would perhaps be *prosocial*— that is, fostering behavior that society generally considers constructive rather than destructive.)

In the mid-1960s, the Children's Television Workshop was created to explore and develop the possibilities for television's *prosocial influence* on children. Using both federal and private funding, it gathered together psychologists, educators, producers, animators, and researchers to dig into everything that was known about television and children. It created pilot projects whose purpose was to accelerate children's learning at an early age (30 to 60 months). The result of their efforts was *Sesame Street*, a program that constructed the environment of the TV child in an entertaining and instructive manner.

Research that has been done on the effects of this prosocial programming have found results that are nothing short of amazing: The more children watched the program, it found, the more rapidly their cognitive skills developed. It did not seem to matter whether the children viewed the program at home or at a nursery school, or whether they were from an urban ghetto or a rural setting, or what their ethnic background was—the results were the same.[12]

Sesame Street has not been the only attempt at prosocial programming. Before that program was developed, *Mister Rogers' Neighborhood* placed conversations and simple social interactions before the very young child. After *Sesame Street* came commercial network programs that attempted prosocial programming by presenting themes of everyday social problems of older children in *Fat Albert and the Cosby Kids;* drama played out in *ABC's Afterschool Specials;* school lessons in commercial-like flashes such as *School-*

house Rock, Grammar Rock, and others that direct vital concepts at schoolchildren through quick quips. Today, some of the Saturday-morning cartoons offer prosocial themes such as the environmentally conscious *Captain Planet.*

Prosocial content has been extended into programming for older audiences as well. Children's Television Workshop itself tried to educate adults, especially those in circles of poverty, about health issues in *Feelin' Good,* but the results were far below expectations and the experiment was abandoned. Adults, it seemed, had already become conditioned to consume television as entertainment, not to be instructed by television in the guise of entertainment. But other carefully formulated programs, subtly designed to present values while adults' cognitive guard was down, have been more successful.

All in the Family was to be prosocial programming to attack bigotry and ethnic prejudice, or so its creator intended. As it turned out, those viewers whose value systems were aligned with that of the protagonist, Archie Bunker, a recognizable bigot, felt that the show reinforced their ideals. Others, less inclined to Archie Bunker's way of thinking, saw the intention of its creator, Norman Lear, as uncovering bigotry and encouraging racial harmony.[13] *Roots: The Next Generation* gave a new appreciation to black culture and helped fortify values of racial harmony and egalitarianism.[14]

A disturbing question nonetheless arose: If program creators can advocate specific values through their programs' characters, is that not being manipulative? And since Americans are typically heavy TV viewers, will television not come to construct individuals' value systems, to the point that television replaces the one-on-one parental tutorials within the family of earlier generations as the source of values education?[15]

While the research conclusions on the effects of prosocial programming efforts were mixed, one thing was certain. An intensive effort had been made to reverse the negative connotations associated with watching television as "wasting time." Strong efforts in both education and the television industry had tried to reconstruct positively the learning experience from television.

Television-watching as an unintended source of values, however, turned out not to be a simple, clear-cut subject. TV-watching per se need not be "wrong," "bad," or unethical. But early on, it was found that television's cumulative effects were mixed, depending on the specific circumstances of viewing and the personal set of values a person brought to the situation. As one commentator summarizes the conclusions,

> So all in all, so far as adult judgments are concerned, television helps to educate the child, but watching it interferes with his education. It helps keep him busy and out of mischief, but it also keeps him too busy to do his chores. It keeps the kids in when you want them in—which is good, except for some of the bad things they see. And it keeps them in when you want them out—which is bad even if they see good things. Ideally, then, TV should provide interesting, educational programs that intrigue children when parents don't want to be bothered with them—but not when they ought to be outside or doing something else.[16]

Perhaps better than any other statement, this conclusion—drawn by Gary Steiner a generation ago, in 1963—demonstrates the ambivalence with which we regard television. Television is all things to all people, nothing to some, and a place to find something for everyone. Today, the increasingly diverse and numerous channels make that even more true. If ever there were an argument for the value of pluralism, it might well be on the side of the television culture.

Nevertheless, even though good things can be seen on television, the *shaping of habits* through television-viewing is still the focus of concern. Such control over behavior begins in early childhood, when most of an individual's cognitive development occurs. Based on such concerns, the child advocacy group Action for Children's Television published these guidelines for parents:

Treat TV with T.L.C.
- Talk about TV with your child! . . .
- Look at TV with your child! . . .
- Choose TV programs with your child! . . .

Such an approach assumes the *family ethic*, the long-held value that parents are responsible for their young children, in everything from providing nourishing food, to instilling prosocial values, and especially to controlling television-viewing. Yet more than a few families diffuse that control to whatever the family members, including the children themselves, want, at nearly any time of the day. (On any given night, well over a million preadolescent children may still be watching TV *at midnight*.) With the changes in family structure in our society, it may well be that we can no longer assume parental responsibility to be as it once was.

SUMMARY

Putting all this into context in a discussion of ethics, we must consider the following:

1. Choosing how a person consumes media, in particular television, and how he or she fills leisure time is indicative of a set of personal values, or a personal ethic.

2. Attitudes toward the extent of people's television viewing, especially toward heavy viewing, reveal both a personal value judgment and a more widespread social concern, or a social ethic.

3. Ideas about television's influence on children come to reflect the values of a family and the parents' responsibilities, even though some parents have only a faint understanding of how television can come to shape the values of their own family.

4. Television's influence on children has become a subject of social, political, economic, and scientific concern. In all this, only brief attention is usually given to the impact of television on children's values.

5. Generally, using leisure time to watch television is a direct consequence of personal and social values held about leisure time and toward television, although often not consciously so.

NOTES

1. Marshall McLuhan, *Understanding Media: The Extensions of Man* (New York: McGraw-Hill, 1964).
2. Jerry Mander, "Four Arguments for the Elimination of Television," in Marie Winn, *The Plug-In Drug* (New York: Viking, 1977).
3. See, for example, Charles Winick, "The Functions of Television: Life Without the Big Box," in S. Oskamp, ed., *Television as a Social Issue* (Thousand Oaks, Ca.: Sage Publications, 1988). *See also* B. H. Ryan, "Would You Free Your Children from the Monster?" *Denver Post*, June 9, 1974. Among the first explorations in this area is Gary Steiner, *The People Look at Television* (New York: Alfred A. Knopf, 1963).

4. Jerry Mander, *Four Arguments for the Elimination of Television* (New York: William Morrow, 1978).

5. From the earliest manuscript of the *Maxims* (the Prisse Papyrus in Paris), translated by R. O. Faulkner. In *The Ancient Egyptian Pyramid Texts*. (Oxford: Clarendon Press, 1969): 11.

6. Benjamin Franklin, *Poor Richard's Almanac,* June 1746.

7. Quoted in Robert Kubey and Mihaly Czikszentmihalyi, *Television and the Quality of Life* (Hillsdale, N.J.: Lawrence Erlbaum Associates, 1990): 21.

8. Robert Hutchins, January 2, 1954, in *International Thesaurus of Quotations* (New York: Crowell, 1970); quoted in Kubey and Czikszentmihalyi, *Television and the Quality of Life*, p. 21.

9. Neil Postman, *Amusing Ourselves to Death* (New York: Viking, 1985): 156, 163.

10. The National Institute of Mental Health published seven studies under the surgeon general's supervision. Five of them have been published as volumes of its series entitled *Television and Social Behavior:* Vol. 1—*Media Content and Control*; Vol. 2—*Television and Social Learning*; Vol. 3—*Television and Adolescent Aggressiveness*; Vol. 4—*Television in Day-to-Day Life: Patterns of Use*; Vol. 5 —*Further Explorations.*

    The other two are *Television and Growing Up: The Impact of Televised Violence* (Reports of the Surgeon General's Scientific Advisory Committee on Television and Social Behavior); and *Television and Social Behavior: An Annotated Bibliography of Research Focusing on Television's Impact on Children.*

11. Remarks of Jesse L. Steinfeld, U.S. Surgeon General, before the Subcommittee on Communications of the Committee on Commerce, U.S. Senate, March 1972.

12. Samuel Ball and Gerry Bogatz, "A Summary of the Major Findings in 'The First Year of Sesame Street: An Evaluation'" (Princeton, N.J.: Educational Testing Service, 1970).

13. N. Vidmar and M. Rokeach, "Archie Bunker's Bigotry: A Study in Selective Perception and Exposure," *Journal of Communication* 24:1 (1974): 36–47

14. See S. J. Ball-Rokeach, J. W. Grube, and M. Rokeach, "'*Roots: The Next Generation*'—Who Watched and with What Effect?" *Public Opinion Quarterly* 45 (1981): 58–68.

15. An excellent discussion of the problems and dilemmas of defining prosocial television with an eye to ethics and values is William J. Brown and Arvind Singhal, "Ethical Dilemmas of Prosocial Television," *Communication Quarterly* 38:3 (Summer 1990): 268–80.

16. Steiner, *People Look at Television*, p. 95.

4

Professional Codes

While radio and television were developing, those responsible for their shaping created a Code of Good Practice, to be overseen by the National Association of Broadcasters. Part of the Television Code, which entailed dozens of pages, indicated that:

- "The exposition of sex crimes will be avoided."
- Care shall be exercised "[i]n avoiding material which is excessively violent or would create morbid suspense, or other undesirable reactions in children."

Case Study 4.1: Copycat Crimes— Can Codes Prevent Them?

In the mid-1970s, NBC aired a television movie, *Born Innocent*, which depicted the rape of a young girl, whose assailants used the handle of a plumber's helper. The program became notorious because of a copycat crime that the show allegedly created. The adolescent perpetrators raped a young girl in much the same way; they had seen *Born Innocent* the night before. The victim brought tort action against NBC and its San Francisco affiliate for showing a crime that resulted in its imitation.[1]

Although courts decided that no fault for the crime rested with the network or stations, the broader questions (apart from the legal one) involve ethics: Should such a crime have been depicted on television in the first place? Should the guidelines articulated in the Television Code be adhered to, even if the language became more lenient? Is there a point at which plots or depictions become unacceptable? If so, where is the line drawn, and who decides where to draw it? Do any guidelines put forth in a professional code have binding force?

These are questions that can guide our discussion through the problem of professional codes. The idea of professional standards of ethics was identified in Chapter 2. Most professionals, such as physicians, lawyers, and psychiatrists, have such guidance. Some codes are nationally recognized for a profession as a whole; others differ from organization to organization. Thus, while there may be no nationally recognized code of business ethics, many individual businesses have their own code of ethics.

In broadcasting, codes have shifted over the years from being the product of a single national association—the National Association of Broadcasters, or NAB—to mostly individual station or network practices. The story of how NAB dropped its code and eventually replaced it with some general guidelines is told below.

Codes may be valuable in aiding in the identification of values held by a profession and how those values evolve over the years. The method of value juxtaposition can be used in comparing earlier codes with later or current ones.

BROADCASTING'S FIRST CODE OF ETHICS

On March 26, 1929, the National Association of Broadcasters held a meeting in Chicago where it adopted the Code of Good Practice, the first code of ethics in radio broadcasting. NAB's president, William Hedges, stated that establishing the Code "was based on keeping radio on a high ethical and moral plane."[2] He indicated that this action was "the most progressive movement that has ever taken place in radio"[3] and that it showed "our desire to do our own house cleaning without waiting for regulation by the government."[4] Hedges also stated, "This action is concrete evidence of the good faith and honest intention of those to whom the government has granted licenses to use this new medium."[5] NAB thus first conceived of the Code as a way of demonstrating that its responsible *self*-regulation was the best alternative to *government* regulation.

The 1929 NAB Code consisted of eight rules. Four of the eight rules governed the use of radio for advertising purposes, revealing the concern over the "problem of commercialization" (see Chapter 2). The first rule prohibited the broadcasting of any matter that would commonly be regarded as offensive because the radio audience included persons of all ages with various religious and social beliefs. Further rules prevented the broadcasting of matter that would be forbidden from the mail as "fraudulent, deceptive or obscene." If it could not be mailed, it could not be aired. Since having a broadcast license is a public trust, a further rule urged broadcasters to screen their personnel carefully so that dishonest or dangerous clients would not obtain access to the public by the use of radio. Another rule explained fair business practices with the competition. A final rule warned that any violation of the Code of Ethics would be investigated and notified.

It became apparent early on that enforcement would be a problem. So what if someone violated the Code? What would be done? Would the station lose its license? No. Would the individual be fined? No. Would they be professionally ostracized? Not really. Enforcement of the Code was simply a matter of people's word of honor.

The rules of the Code named so far do not seem out of line with contemporary expectations of what such a code might contain. But half of the Code was devoted to advertising practices—and there one finds a stark contrast with today's practices.

BROADCAST ETHICS AND COMMERCIAL TIME LIMITS

The Code recognized the dual function of radio: daytime companionship and business before six o'clock in the evening, and relaxing nighttime listening, often as a family, after six o'clock. Almost apologetically, the Code noted, "Time before 6 P.M. . . . may be devoted in part, at least, to broadcasting programs of a business nature; while time after 6 P.M. is for recreation and relaxation, and commercial programs should be of the good-will type. Commercial announcements, as the term is generally understood, *should not* be broadcast between 7 and 11 P.M."[6]

Whatever ethics might be involved in not offending listeners by too much commercialism, however, disappeared with the necessity of economic survival from advertising, evening hours or

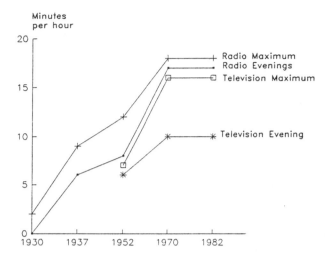

FIGURE 4.1 Commercial Time Allowed by NAB Code

not. By 1937, the NAB Code allowed a maximum of 9 minutes of commercial material per daytime hour and only 6 minutes each evening hour, soon to be known as "prime time." In 1970, the Radio Code permitted twice that much—18 minutes per hour, day or night.

In television, the trend grew much the same way: for daytime TV, from 7 minutes per hour to 16 minutes in 1970; during prime time, from 6 minutes to 10 minutes. (See Figure 4.1.) (What these numbers do not reflect is the increase in the number of commercials, since in 1970 most commercials were 60 seconds long, with some 30-second commercials. Today, many commercials are only 10 or 20 seconds long; few go as long as 60 seconds anymore. Thus, the possibility exists of being exposed to three or four times as many commercials as before.)

The increase in advertising time in radio and television seems to have gone mostly unnoticed by listeners and viewers, at least through formal complaint. Some radio stations now promote themselves as "more music" stations—presumably with less advertising. But for some stations this idea seems to have been prompted less by complaining listeners than by advertisers who were concerned that their commercials were getting lost in a maze of "advertising clutter."

One group, however, lobbied broadcasters strongly on the issue of advertising in children's television. Action for Children's

Television (ACT) first spoke out against any advertising at all that was directed to children: "Why should you be allowed to sell directly to my child?" ACT asked. "I don't let door-to-door salesmen do it. The child has virtually no purchasing power, so you're encouraging the child to pester his/her parents into buying the products you advertise. It isn't fair."

ACT never was successful in removing advertising completely from children's programs. And for good reason—the broadcasters pointed out that commercials were what pays for these programs: "No advertising targeted toward children, no children's programs!" Even so, ACT thought that broadcasters should pay for children's programs through their general profits—that is, that children's television should be sustained programming.

Finally, by early 1990, Congress passed the Children's Television Act. A compromise was struck: ceilings of 12 minutes of kid-vid advertising per hour on weekdays, 10.5 minutes on weekends. As it turns out, the time limits are now higher than the networks currently run, although some local stations may push or exceed these limits.

Ethics are intimately bound up with time limits for advertising in radio and television. This has been the case since 1929, and it is the case today. There is something "unethical" about too much commercialization. Listeners and viewers realize it; broadcasters sense it.

In 1982 time limits for advertising were still in place, when the ethics of time limits clashed with another legal (and ethical) issue: that of too much control, possibly manipulating competition.

Case Study 4.2: NAB's Dilemma— Drop the Code or Litigate?

The Code of Ethics for broadcasters has served as a restraint on advertising. In the late 1970s the three major networks—ABC, CBS, and NBC—were in the heyday of their popularity, wealth and influence. Conforming to the NAB Code, however, the networks had policies in place that interfered with the plans of some advertisers.

The Code prohibited "piggybacking"—displaying more than one product commercial within a purchased timeframe of less than 60 seconds. The Code limited the number of commercial interruptions per program, the number of consecutive announcements per interruption, and the total amount of advertising time per hour.

One network advertiser, Alberto-Culver, was seeking larger time blocks for its commercials on the three networks. But the Code made it difficult for Alberto-Culver and many other advertisers to get the kind of advertising schedule they wished from the networks.[7]

Because of the Code's restraining influence, Alberto-Culver asked the U.S. Justice Department to determine whether it violated antitrust laws concerning *restraint of trade*. The government agreed that it did, and a consent decree was issued to the networks. The "big three" networks were reluctant to violate the Code of Good Practice and indicated to the courts that they were bound by their professional standards. This noncompliance resulted in a court challenge in U.S. District Court.

Finally, in March 1982, Federal District Court Judge Harold Greene determined that the Code's time restraints were subordinate to the federal antitrust laws. Judge Greene did not believe that broadcasting's trusteeship of the public's airwaves was best maintained through self-regulation, such as in the NAB Codes:

> The Congress has determined where the public interest lies when antitrust liability is at issue: it lies in free and fair competition . . . If there are to be exceptions from that policy in favor of other, different public interest considerations, they must be made by Congress.[8]

Further, he noted that the Code was not wholly self-regulation, in that it was part of a contractual arrangement to which NAB members are obliged to adhere.

Interestingly enough, as early as 1961, NAB anticipated that its Code's time standards might be seen as antitrust violations and restraint of trade. A query to the Justice Department about such a potential violation brought the response that the Antitrust Division was

> sympathetic to the ends you are trying to achieve in elevating the level of broadcasting programming and commercials to comport with these standards of good taste and ethical conduct set forth in the Codes and . . . such goals would appear to be both commendable and in the public interest.[9]

Two decades later, however, the Justice Department took a different position in going to court. Courts are, of course, a place where disputes are settled. Each side in a dispute may have good and intelligent arguments. The duty of the judge is to make a decision, based on what he or she interprets as the law taking the highest priority. In this case, Judge Greene decided that laws concerning antitrust and restraint of trade practices were more important than opportunities for self-regulation and ethical practices.

> Do you agree? What are the values on each side of this argument? What could be the consequences if the broadcasters' code of ethics were voided? What would be the consequences if big business avoided all "restraints of trade" and all government checks? Does it have to be all one way or the other? Is there room for some kind of "golden mean" here (see Chapter 2)?

NAB understood the government's position on antitrust violations, so it returned to court with a compromise: NAB would agree not to enforce certain Code provisions, and the government would agree not to object to an order from the appeals court dismissing as moot and vacating Greene's earlier decision.[10]

Finally, in November of 1982, NAB agreed to drop the Code entirely. It made little sense to keep it if it could not enforce its provisions. It was at this point that groups began to speak out, concerned about the loss of ethical guidelines for broadcasters. Action for Children's Television, for example, was concerned about the cancellation of passages related to children's programming.

In a footnote in the case, the court had hinted that nothing in its decree "restricts the ability of television stations, each acting on its own, or under pressure from organizations such as ACT, to implement advertising policies that seek to balance program and non-program material in a reasonable and responsible manner."[11] The court thus seemed interested only in potential *antitrust* violations of the code, and it suggested that marketplace forces— including self-regulation—be permitted to control nonantitrust considerations.

Since only about 22 percent of the Code addressed limits on advertising time and placement restrictions that were of concern to the court in this case, groups like ACT argued, why not keep a modified Code instead of throwing it out entirely? Why not keep the other 78 percent and throw out only those parts that violated antitrust? Why throw out the baby with the bathwater?

ARGUMENTS FOR AND AGAINST THE CODE

There would seem to be sound arguments for both dropping and keeping the Code.[12]

Arguments for Dropping the Code

1. The public is not best served by a professionwide standard in which the public generally has little say. The public would be better served by standards of ethics that are implemented by local stations responsive to local market interests. The level of responsiveness would be better at the local station level than nationally, especially in our diverse pluralistic society, where one community (market) may be much different from another.

2. NAB and the industry as a whole have much to gain from no longer worrying about the Code—constantly modifying, adding and updating it. Moreover, the difficult problem of enforcing the Code would no longer be a burden on the industry, since it was a broadcaster's good faith and honesty that made the Code work anyway, not external or industrywide enforcement.

3. Stations and networks will enjoy larger profits if they can ease upward the number of advertising minutes per hour. The public, after all, hardly has noticed that the networks and stations have already gradually increased the number of commercial minutes per hour. (It should be noted, however, that since the 1982 case, stations and networks generally have not increased the advertising time. This may be due, however, to the fact that network advertising schedules are lighter because of increased competition from cable and other advertising media. The "big three" are not all that big anymore. But greater financial advantage seemed to be *promised* as a result of the end of the Code.)

4. There will be more freedom for individual stations, networks, and program creators without the Code. After all, themes that were once sensitive have become subjects of everyday conversation. Writers and producers will be free to address such pressing social issues, unrestricted by the Code, which reflected earlier, more conservative values.

Arguments for Keeping the Code

1. Nationally visible codes serve to educate program creators, news writers, and business practitioners on the general profes-

sional expectations concerning their roles. The NAB Code—which actually contained a code for radio and a code for television—was comprehensive, detailing everything from program standards to responsibilities toward children, from treatment of news and controversial public issues to advertising claims. Codes provide a true focus on ethics—on proper (conventional) and improper (unacceptable) ways of doing things. No special, arduous training was necessary for work performed with an eye to the Code.

2. Adherence to the Code was good public relations. It could earn a broadcaster a Seal of Good Practice that it could then display or declare on the air, letting viewers or listeners know of the station's strict compliance to professional ethics. Code membership itself was once considered a positive influence in the broadcasting community. At the apex of its use, in the mid-1960s, the then–president of NAB, Vince Wasilewski, indicated, "Our Codes are not peripheral activities. No activity of NAB is closer to the public."[13]

3. The Code served as a source of prestige for broadcasters among professional associates. The implication was that those who subscribed to the Code and displayed the Seal took their mission of broadcasting as a serious responsibility, both self-imposed and professionally expected. In 1966 the Code stated two aims: "To embody a set of professional standards that reflect broadcaster service to the public. To maintain and preserve the freedom of self-determination."[14]

4. Adherence to the Code was a way of demonstrating that a broadcaster fulfilled the public service responsibility expected by the FCC. A broadcaster who stuck to the Code would probably be pretty safe at license renewal time. The FCC intuitively felt that adherence to the Code guidelines demonstrated responsibility. The industry's self-policing was doing what the government might otherwise have had to do in checking on responsible conduct.

THE NEW NAB STATEMENT: FROM THE RESTRICTIVE TO THE ADVISORY

The dozen or so pages of the old NAB Code contained a long, detailed list of prohibitions against programming that was thought to be inappropriate. For example: "The creation of a state of hypnosis by act or detailed demonstration on camera is prohibited and hypnosis as a form of 'parlor game' antics to create humorous situations within a comedy setting is forbidden."[15]

Other prohibitions listed included showing criminal techniques; presenting the use of illegal drugs as appropriate; ridiculing those who suffer from physical or mental afflictions or deformities; showing obscene, profane, or indecent material; running programs of fortune-telling, occultism, astrology, and the like; and presenting dramatized material as news.

These were just the prohibitions that involved programming. Other sections of the Code dealt with the treatment of news and public events, controversial public issues, political telecasts, religious programs, and advertising standards.

This list of prohibitions, which had been assiduously constructed, was gone with the dropping of the Code. For eight years, from 1982 to 1990, the NAB had no guidelines, although various networks and stations had their own.

The absence of standards on a national scale bothered some observers, including some ethics-minded broadcasters. In July 1990, NAB announced a new Statement of Principles of Radio and Television Broadcasting:

> The Board issues this statement of principles to record and reflect what it believes to be the generally accepted standards of America's radio and television broadcasters. Many broadcasters now have written standards of their own. All have their own programming policies. NAB would hope that all broadcasters would set down in writing their general programming principles and policies, as the Board hereby sets down the following principles.[16]

The new Statement focused more on having broadcasters "exercise responsible and careful judgment in the selection of material for broadcast" than on forming a list of prohibitions. Cautions in dealing with violence, drugs and substance abuse, and sexually oriented material, however, were specifically mentioned as "specific program principles." Two special responsibilities were identified as well:

- Responsibly exercised artistic freedom.
- Responsibility in children's programming.

Unlike many professional codes, the new Statement of Principles was "of necessity general and advisory, rather than specific and restrictive." And being genuinely advisory, there was to be "no interpretation or enforcement of these principles by NAB or others."[17] The Statement was intended to reflect rather than project social mores: "not . . . to establish new criteria for programming decisions, but rather to reflect generally accepted practices of America's radio and television programmers."[18]

Finally, the new Statement reflected concern for First Amendment considerations:

> Both NAB and the stations it represents respect and defend the individual broadcaster's First Amendment rights to select and present programming according to its individual assessment of the desires and expectations of its audiences and of the public interest.[19]

BROADCASTERS' NEED FOR PROFESSIONAL ETHICS

During the eight-year vacuum, when there was no national code of professional ethics, how did broadcasters feel about the situation? The answer to this question can be partly found in a survey taken during those eight years.

In a survey of readers of *Electronic Media* in the fall of 1987, respondents indicated concern over some ethical practices in broadcasting: "One-sided news reporting, poor quality news reporting, business pressure on news programs . . . and plain, old-fashioned deception and lying" were mentioned among broadcasters' concerns.[20]

When asked, "Do you believe that the development of a comprehensive code of ethics would help with hyping (during sweeps months in order to boost ratings) and other controversial practices?" half the respondents answered yes.

On the inherent ethical dilemma that broadcasters face by virtue of their public service responsibilities and their need to earn a profit: "In your opinion, are the goals of profit and public service sometimes in conflict?" Seventy-three percent replied yes; 27 percent replied no.

An even more direct and pragmatic question was posed: "Would you run an informative, public service program over one with solely entertainment value even if it hurt the bottom line?" The answers:

Yes, frequently: 22 percent

Yes, but infrequently: 72 percent

No, never: 5 percent

Generally, respondents felt that the *rhetoric* of business ethics exceeded the *reality* for most companies, by an 80 to 20 percent margin.

Among many other points, respondents felt that balance was the best approach in working the ethical dilemmas. Eighty-five percent felt that the statement that best characterized the social responsibility of a business manager was: "The social responsibility of business is to weigh and help satisfy the interests of a number of 'stakeholders' such as investors, consumers and employees."

In analyzing the results of the survey, Tom Donaldson, Wirtenberger Professor of Ethics at Loyola University in Chicago, concluded that the respondents "showed overwhelming confidence in the statement that 'generally speaking, good ethics is good business.'"

Donaldson also cited surveys that showed that "those companies that ranked highest in ethics also tended to rank highest in growth in earnings per share over a seven-year period. Over the last 30 years, the 'high ethics' companies experienced a 23-fold increase in value compared to an average Dow Jones Industrial Average increase of five-fold."

Case Study 4.3: Self-Survey—Ethics in Management

For the following survey, you may either assume you have a management position in broadcasting, or you may take it from a consumer's perspective. Note your responses, then compare them with the results of a national sample.

Q 1. The NAB Television Code was eliminated in 1982. How familiar were you with this code?

    (a) Very familiar

    (b) Somewhat familiar

    (c) A little familiar

    (d) Not at all familiar

Q 2. How much change have you seen since 1982 in the ethical standards of your station and in the industry as a whole?

		Station	*Industry*
(a)	Many changes	1	1
(b)	Some changes	2	2
(c)	Little change	3	3
(d)	No change	4	4

Q 3. Have the rules and principles changed at your station since 1982 for each of the following?

(a)	treatment of news events	yes	no
(b)	community responsibility	yes	no
(c)	program content standards	yes	no
(d)	children's programming standards	yes	no
(e)	business practices	yes	no
(f)	advertising standards	yes	no
(g)	commercial time per hour	yes	no
(h)	no. of commercials per hour	yes	no

Q 4. Does your station have its own standard of practices for:

(a)	treatment of news events	yes	no
(b)	community responsibility	yes	no
(c)	program content standards	yes	no
(d)	children's programming standards	yes	no
(e)	business practices	yes	no
(f)	advertising standards	yes	no
(g)	commercial time per hour	yes	no
(h)	no. of commercials per hour	yes	no

Q 5. Do you think that each of these sections of the former NAB Code should be retained in a new code?

(a)	treatment of news events	yes	no
(b)	community responsibility	yes	no
(c)	program content standards	yes	no
(d)	children's programming standards	yes	no
(e)	business practices	yes	no
(f)	advertising standards	yes	no
(g)	commercial time per hour	yes	no
(h)	no. of commercials per hour	yes	no

Q 6. Do you think most individual stations are currently regulating themselves?   yes   no

Q 7. Do you think there is a problem with
the direction of professional ethical
practices in the broadcasting industry?   yes   no

Q 8. If the industry does not regulate itself
with regard to ethical practices, do
you think government will impose
regulation?   yes   no

Q 9. Do you think government should impose regulations in each
of these areas?

(a)	treatment of news events	yes	no
(b)	community responsibility	yes	no
(c)	program content standards	yes	no
(d)	children's programming standards	yes	no
(e)	business practices	yes	no
(f)	advertising standards	yes	no
(g)	commercial time per hour	yes	no
(h)	no. of commercials per hour	yes	no

Q 10. At which level do you think industry standards and practices
should be regulated?
  (a) Individual station level
  (b) National Association of Broadcasters
  (c) Some other group (e.g., NATPE, RTNDA, etc.)
  (d) New national body representing stations

Q 11. If a code of ethics were to be enacted again, how would you
like to see it be enforced?
  (a) No provision for enforcement (entirely voluntary)
  (b) Public censoring
  (c) Membership revocation in code

Q 12. If a national, self-regulatory code were
created, would your station adhere
to it?   yes   no

Q 13. Do you feel ethical standards limit the
free and competitive American system
of broadcasting?   yes   no

Q 14. Generally, how do you feel the issue of ethical standards
should be addressed by the broadcast industry? (explain
briefly)

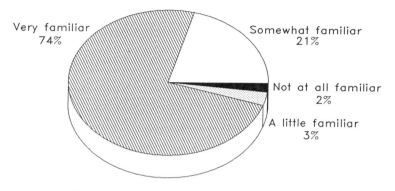

FIGURE 4.2 Familiarity with the Old NAB Code

This survey questionnaire was sent by mail to station managers in the largest 20 markets (or city areas) and markets 61–80 in the spring of 1989. The findings were as follows:

1. Managers were generally familiar with the previous code (74.2 percent) (see Figure 4.2).

2. While station managers saw few, if any changes in ethical standards at their own stations (76.6 percent), they saw several changes in the industry as a whole (67.2 percent) (see Figure 4.3).

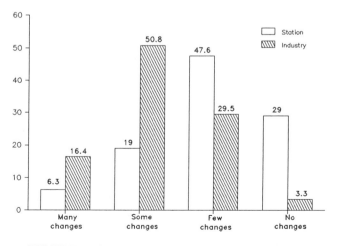

FIGURE 4.3 Perceived Changes in Standards

3. While only a few stations had changed their own principles governing news and programming, about half had brought
about changes in their advertising standards of commercial time
per hour (see Figures 4.4 and 4.5).

4. Most stations (95 percent) had some kind of their own
standards and practices for news programming and advertising
(see Figure 4.6).

5. About half of the respondents felt that standards relating
to practices of news, programming, and advertising ought to be
retained in a new national code or ethical standard (see Figure 4.7).

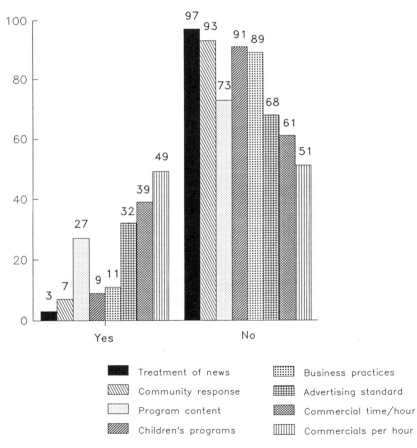

FIGURE 4.4 Changes in Standards

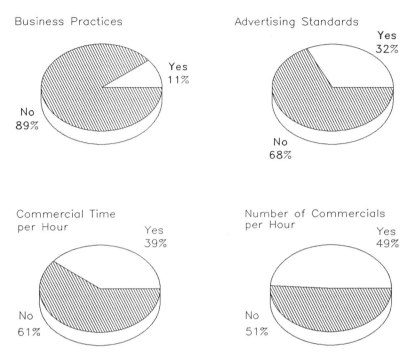

Business Practices

Yes
11%

No
89%

Advertising Standards

Yes
32%

No
68%

Commercial Time
per Hour

Yes
39%

No
61%

Number of Commercials
per Hour

Yes
49%

No
51%

FIGURE 4.5   Changes in Standards—Advertising

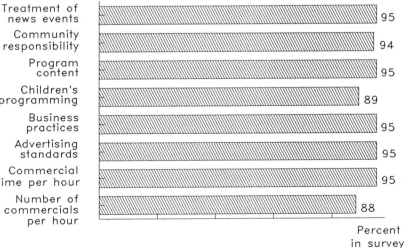

Treatment of news events	95
Community responsibility	94
Program content	95
Children's programming	89
Business practices	95
Advertising standards	95
Commercial time per hour	95
Number of commercials per hour	88

Percent
in survey

FIGURE 4.6   Stations with These Standards

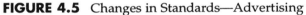

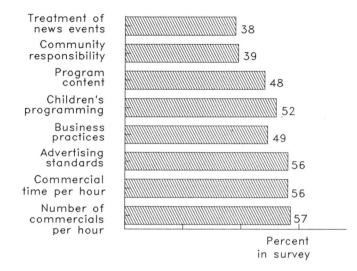

FIGURE 4.7 Standards That Should Be Retained in New Code

6. Forty percent were uncertain whether individual stations were currently regulating themselves (see Figure 4.8).

7. Twenty-seven percent of station managers thought there was a problem with the direction of professional ethical practices in the broadcasting industry (see Figure 4.9).

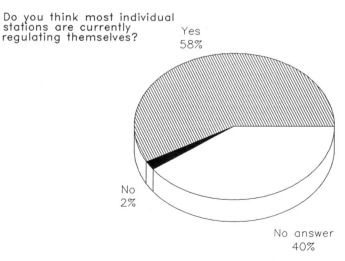

FIGURE 4.8 Current Self-regulation

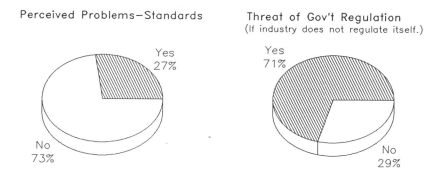

Perceived Problems—Standards

Threat of Gov't Regulation
(If industry does not regulate itself.)

FIGURE 4.9 Broadcast Regulation: Directions and Threats

8. While almost no one thought there should be government regulation in news, programming, or advertising, 71 percent felt that if the industry *did not regulate* itself with regard to ethical practices, the *government would* impose regulations (see Figure 4.9).

9. Respondents felt strongly that the government should *not* impose standards in all areas queried (see Figure 4.10).

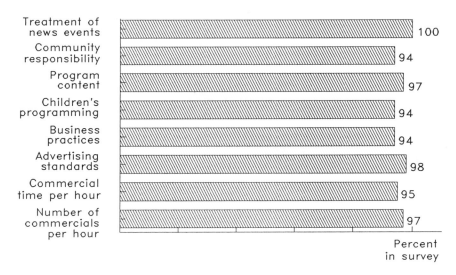

FIGURE 4.10 Should Government Impose Standards?

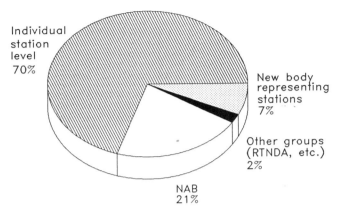

FIGURE 4.11   Where Should Practices Be Regulated?

10.   Most respondents (69.6 percent) felt that ethical standards were best regulated at the individual station level, but 21.4 percent felt that this should be an NAB task (see Figure 4.11).

11.   On how a national code should be enforced, 56.6 percent thought adherence should be entirely voluntary; 37.1 percent thought it should be enforced by the sanction of revocation of code membership; and 6.5 percent thought public censorship was the best means of enforcement (see Figure 4.12).

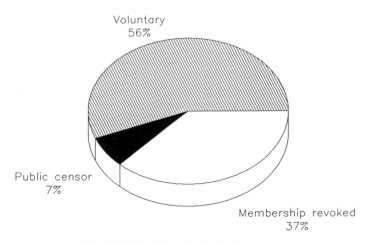

FIGURE 4.12   Code Enforcement

12. If a national self-regulatory code were created, 92 percent of station managers felt their station would adhere to it.

13. Finally, 77 percent felt that ethical standards *do not* limit the free and competitive American system of broadcasting (see Figure 4.13).[21]

The last finding seems to concur with Donaldson's assertion that there need not be a conflict between good, profitable business practices and the forthright practice of ethics. As a matter of fact, "Good ethics is good business."

During the eight-year hiatus, then, there seemed to be some momentum among broadcasters for a code of ethics—a visible set of professional standards. They felt that the public, as well as those who work day-to-day in radio and television, should know that broadcasting worked by some standards of practice.

The key question nonetheless remained: How could the industry have a code of ethics without usurping the creative freedom of those on the frontier of controversial social themes, or of those handling hot news items with a visual medium that was still finding its forms of expression?

The NAB Board of Directors faced this dilemma in the new Statement of Principles, discussed above. To many broadcasters, the Statement seemed an appropriate compromise. It addressed the problem of artistic freedom, while advising about sensitivity to

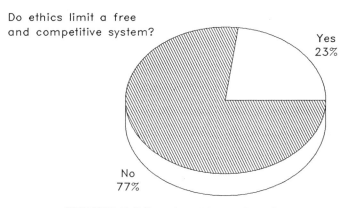

FIGURE 4.13 Ethics Versus Freedom

potentially exploitative themes. It articulated concern only about the most controversial themes: violence, substance abuse, sexually oriented material, and children's programming. It left a lot unsaid. And most notably, it emphasized its advisory nature; there was no provision for any kind of enforcement.

Will the Statement ultimately be found satisfactory? That question may not be answered until a measure of time can be used to assess its value.

There are other codes that affect broadcasting practices. Those involved in reporting news may be guided more by the Radio/ Television News Directors Association Code of Broadcast News Ethics, a two-page, eleven-article code that addresses itself to news practices (see Chapter 7). It may be noteworthy that this code may work independently of guidance from NAB or, very often, from any station or parent company, which may be more concerned with business practices, programming, or advertising, leaving some leeway for news practices.

Also addressing itself to news practices—in radio, TV, and other news media—is the long-existing code of the Society of Professional Journalists (formerly Sigma Delta Chi), subtitled Journalists' Responsibilities, Obligations (see Chapter 7).

There are other guidelines that a station may follow. A sales staff may conduct its business with an eye to the Advertising Code of American Business. Or the station's administration may work under the Code of Professional Standards for the Practice of Public Relations.

The most publicly familiar code may be the Rating Code of the Motion Picture Association of America, consisting of its ratings of G, PG, PG-13, R, NC-17, and X. While these may not be overtly used in broadcast television, they may still be used by viewers in their selection of movies in premium, pay cable channels. They may also give some guidance to TV program directors who are considering airing movies and movie packages (usually in edited form).

Thus, there does continue to be guidance from ethical principles in the broadcasting industry. No one works in a complete vacuum of values and social mores, least of all broadcasters. What is of interest here is how visibly those ethical applications work in the day-to-day practice in the many levels of broadcasting.

NOTES

1. Olivia N. *v.* NBC, 7 *Med.L.Rptr.* 2359 (1981).
2. "Broadcasters Seek to Clean Up the Industry and Hope to Regulate Commercial Activities on the Air," *New York Times,* Apr. 7, 1929.
3. Ibid.
4. "National Broadcasters Meet at Chicago and Adopt Code of Ethics," *New York Times,* Mar. 26, 1929.
5. "Broadcasters Seek to Clean Up."
6. Llewellyn White, *The American Radio* (Chicago: University of Chicago Press, 1947).
7. Alberto-Culver Co. *v.* National Association of Broadcasters, N1. 83-2327 (D.D.C. filed Nov. 17, 1983): 12–13.
8. U.S. *v.* NAB, 8 *Med.L.Rptr.* 1185 (March 1982).
9. "NAB Says Suit Against TV Code Lacks Substance," *NAB Highlights,* Oct. 15, 1979.
10. U.S. *v.* NAB, 8 *Med.L.Rptr.* 2572 (Nov. 1982).
11. Ibid., 2575.
12. These arguments are outlined in Val Limburg, "The Decline of Broadcast Ethics: U.S. v. NAB," *Journal of Mass Media Ethics* 4:2 (1989): 214–31.
13. National Association of Broadcasters, *The Challenge of Self-Regulation* (Washington, D.C., 1966).
14. NAB Television Code, 1966, *Broadcasting Yearbook* (Washington, D.C.: Broadcasting Publications, 1966).
15. NAB Television Code, 1981, sec. 4, "Special Program Standards," para. 9, as published in *Broadcasting Cable Yearbook* (Washington, D.C.: Broadcasting Publications, 1981): D16.
16. NAB, July 9, 1990 (press release or directive to member stations).
17. Ibid.
18. Ibid.
19. Ibid.
20. "Ethical Dilemmas," *Electronic Media* (Feb. 29, 1988): 1, 48. All quotations from this survey are taken from this article, as are Tom Donaldson's comments.
21. This survey, conducted in February and March 1989, was sent to 167 stations in two market sizes: largest 20 and stations in market size 61–80. The response rate was 42 percent. The data were reported in a paper delivered to the American Journalism History Association, Coeur d'Alene, Idaho, in October 1990.

5

Radio Programming and Values

Radio allows listeners to specialize in some niche of culture. When it comes to music, most listeners stay in their comfort zone. Country music fans listen to little else. Popular music involves several species of rock 'n' roll, but many listeners stick with only one kind: rap, heavy metal, soft rock, album-oriented rock, and so on.

It is easy to program a radio station: Just pick some format of music to play, and insert the commercials, weather, time, and some chatter, right? But what appears to be simple has problems.

Some people who tire of the world of music engage in "parasocial interaction" by listening in on the conversations of talk-radio hosts and hostesses. The talk-radio genre of programming, in turn, has spawned the subgenre of "shock radio," where popular radio hosts speak of subjects not heretofore discussed on the air.

These programs' ratings are often high—some regular radio listeners, particularly those who stick to a single musical format, may be surprised to learn that the most popular radio program in the nation's largest city, New York, is that of Howard Stern.

Howard Stern? Isn't that the "shock jock" whom the FCC fined and censored? Correct. And its reasons for doing so present a compelling and controversial case study in ethics and broadcasting.

SHOCK RADIO: HOWARD STERN

In an era when bold, provocative talk attracts attention—that is, larger audiences—"shock radio" has become a good money-maker for radio stations. When more than one station uses the strategy, the jock with the most outrageous expressions and ideas seems to gain an edge on the competition. This formula for success is a far cry from the original intent of the Federal Criminal Code, which warns of severe penalties to "whoever utters any obscene, indecent, or profane language by means of radio communication."[1]

Just what is the substance of such shock radio?

- After Amy Fisher, the adolescent charged with the attempted murder of her lover's wife, appeared on a TV tabloid show, Stern commented: "I wanted her to take off her clothes."
- On interracial sex, he said: "The closest I came to making love to a black woman was, I masturbated to a picture of Aunt Jemima."
- On Connie Chung, Stern remarked while interviewing her husband, Maury Povich: "For an Oriental woman, she has got big breasts."
- Program segments have included "Bestiality Dial-a-Date."
- After the FCC announced that it was fining a station that carried his program $105,000 for indecent material, Stern said he prayed for the death of FCC chairman Alfred Sikes.
- Women accuse Stern of misogyny, for saying that women like to be raped or abused. His listening audience understandably consists mostly of young white males.[2]

The list could go on, but the point is clear.

Case Study 5.1: "Offensive, Indecent"— But It Makes Money!

Howard Stern's program is highly popular. Several cities now carry the morning show; it is quickly becoming the country's most popular morning drive-time program, moving from a local to a national format. His material, however, often violates FCC indecency standards, and few would argue that it is far from "ethical." Indeed, the cost of the program's popularity may be respect and professional ethics itself.

To some people, if a program makes money, it is a smashing success—that's all there is to it. When I was discussing the ethical nature of Stern's material that it carries with Mel Karmazin, President of Infinity Broadcasting, I was asked: "What's the problem?" He implied that those who believed Stern's material to be indecent had prudish values. He acted insulted that I should even bring up the question of ethics. Since then, Stern and the broadcasting company have been fined over $1 million by the FCC.[3]

Perhaps, then, the question is less where to draw the line in regard to ethical proprieties than whether there is a line at all. Is there a line? If so, where does one trace it when mapping out the territories of ethics? This is especially problematic when one tries to define the domain of social morality, together with the media ethics that reflect that morality.

If you were manager of a station that had an offer to carry Howard Stern's show, would you do it?

There are other complicated questions that go with this, but before they're posed, let's examine another program.

TALK RADIO: RUSH LIMBAUGH

Another New York station, WABC-AM, features Rush Limbaugh, whose rhetoric draws listeners out of humor, rage, or merely curiosity. The unique character of his chatter has drawn a national audience; he is carried by another 400 radio stations around the country. His patter has included:

- Deriding the NAACP director by imitating his voice to sound like *Amos 'n' Andy's* Kingfish.
- Running "news flashes" about the plight of Pee-wee Herman, with the song "Beat It" as background music.
- Calling feminists "femi-nazis," and imputing their activities to the motivation that "they can't get a man, and their rage is one long PMS attack."
- Calling liberals, in their do-good attempts, "commie libs." Limbaugh holds Senator Edward Kennedy in pseudo-fear and ridicule. On Kennedy's criticisms of Supreme Court nominee Clarence Thomas, Limbaugh commented: "Here we have Senator Teddy Kennedy crossing another bridge, this one ideologi-

cal. Will he get across it, or will he take someone down with him again?"

- Cutting off listeners who disagree with his views on abortion with the sounds of a vacuum cleaner and a woman screaming.

Still, the more Limbaugh insults, the bigger his audience gets. The reasons for his popularity—perhaps a sympathetic silent "middle America," or perhaps a curiosity about what outrageous thing he will say next—could easily become the subject for a study in social psychology.

Case Study 5.2: To Carry Rush Limbaugh or Not?

Assume you are a station manager carrying the Limbaugh show. You receive storms of protest about it, and advertisers threaten to boycott. Moreover, the FCC indicates that some material on the show may threaten your station's license, since it seems to violate §1464 of federal statutes prohibiting the broadcasting of profane, obscene, or indecent programming.

Would you curtail the material in any way? Would you censor some of that which may be objectionable? Or would you cut off Limbaugh's show entirely? The dilemma is whether to allow this brassy, insulting, and often distasteful stuff on the air or impose some kind of control at the risk of censorship.

A DECISION BASED ON VALUES ANALYSIS

Before you decide whether to carry a program like Rush Limbaugh's, or even Howard Stern's, based on your first impressions, think through the problem with an analysis of values.

Values That Favor Keeping the Program

Popularity

Rush Limbaugh's program is listened to by hundreds of thousands, perhaps millions of people every day. In a democracy (here, a "cultural democracy"), we tend to respect the will of the people. While this is not a political ballot, these listeners are voting by tuning their radios to Limbaugh's program. What right does anyone have to censor such popularity?

Financial

Such large numbers of listeners translate into income and profit for stations that carry the program, for the advertisers whose products' virtues receive exposure, and most of all, for Limbaugh himself, who gleans a handsome salary for his efforts. Why would a station even think about curbing such a lucrative enterprise, especially at a time when the economy is not all that healthy anyway?

The Problem of Censorship

In a society that deeply believes in free speech and First Amendment rights, it is anathema to prevent someone from uttering even insulting and distasteful stuff. Besides, where does one draw the line as to what might and might not be suitable for censoring? And most basic of all, who does the censoring?

Changing Values

FCC rules and some listeners may find certain materials objectionable, but our pluralistic society is changing and what was once taboo might now be acceptable. There needs to be social recognition of such value shifts.

Values That Favor Controlling the Program

Decency

As evasive as the ideal of decency is, most people accede to the idea that civilized society sets boundaries on acceptable conduct. We still do not see much public nudity or copulation out in the open, for example, despite relaxing standards of sexual mores. Everyone draws a line somewhere as to what is decent, although they may draw it in different places. In public displays of values through broadcasting, station licensees have traditionally been held responsible for the content of the programs their station broadcasts.

Law

Federal law prohibits the broadcasting of any material that is obscene, indecent, or profane (18 U.S.C.A. §1464). Violators may be fined or imprisoned or both. Although what Limbaugh does may not constitute the kind of "indecent" material that is illegal, the "spirit of the law" may be applicable here. On the other hand, some eager attorney may successfully defend Limbaugh, even with considerable time and expense.

Incursion of Privacy

Many people argue that listeners have the right not to have to be exposed to such material. In 1970 the U.S. Supreme Court indicated, "Nothing in the Constitution compels us to listen to or view any unwanted communication, whatever its merit."[4] One may counter that if one does not like Limbaugh or any particular communication, he or she may simply turn off the radio. To that comes the reply that radio, like drinking water, is so pervasive that responsibility lies with the sender, much as a family assumes that drinking water is rendered suitable for consumption before it is pumped through the community.

Professional Standards

Among broadcasters there are professional standards of conduct. Although the NAB's original Code was discontinued, then integrated into a new Statement of Principles (see Chapter 4), expectations of professional standards still remain. Agreed-upon norms guide what professionals consider to be appropriate standards. To ignore them may put the violator into the category of a "nonprofessional," or someone without ethics. The consequence may be the stigma of being professionally unethical.

Making the Decision

These are but some of the arguments that assist in the analysis of the Limbaugh and Stern case studies and the problems of latitude and tolerance versus control or censorship that they reflect. These cases reveal two conflicting sets of values: one for keeping the programs, one for controlling the programs. Many observers' ethics embrace values on both sides of the issue. For any given individual, which side takes priority may have to do with his or her basic philosophy or ground rules of ethics.

The Limbaugh case in particular exemplifies other basic dilemmas as well:

convention/tradition	versus	progress/liberality
regulation/social control	versus	individual freedom
discipline/strictness	versus	tolerance/ broadmindedness
respect/courtesy	versus	daring/creativity
discipline/self-control	versus	innovation/free-form
social approbation/respect	versus	independence/ eclecticism

The list could go on. But the point is that values, important as they may be, often come into direct conflict with other values, which may also have a high priority for an individual, a professional group, or a society.

To what extent do we consider "daring, leading edge" artistic expression permissible for the public as a whole if it seems to also be "obscene"? The virtue of tolerance may be strained under the test of this next case study.

Case Study 5.3: 2-Live Crew

A relatively obscure rap music group, 2-Live Crew, has gained the limelight. Its heavy use of taboo expressions—something that other musical artists have only toyed with—has resulted in attention being drawn to them. The group produced an album, *As Nasty as They Wanna Be*, whose rhythms are compelling but whose lyrics often seem incredible. "Did I really hear what I think I just heard?" stunned listeners ask themselves. A textual analysis of the album reveals the following:

- use of the "F-word": 226 times
- use of *bitch*: 163 times
- references to genitalia, male and female: 117 times
- references to oral sex: 87 times
- references to buttocks (mostly female): 43 times

In one instance local law enforcement has prosecuted the group for a live performance violating local obscenity laws. At least for one brief moment in history, 2-Live Crew is "hot."

The attention drawn to the group makes its album a natural for the playlist of the radio station for which you are program director. Do you put 2-Live Crew on your playlist, making your station the "bold" one in your market, striking out progressively, while your competitors remain on their backsides? Attention, ratings, and subsequent increased profits for your radio station may be the result of this action.

Perhaps, on the other hand, there is popular progressive clamor to hear the album in your area. If the language and ideas expressed seem wrong in your value system, should you impose your more traditional values here? And aside from the possible regulatory violations in airing some obscenity, as defined in federal law, what is actually wrong with responding to popular trends? In this case combinations of rap music and raw language seem to be a cultural trend.

How do you determine the posture of your personal values in relation to trends that reflect a sizable or growing number of listeners? Your decision will necessarily reflect your own value system. Can you defend your value system?

THE SHOCK OF CREATIVE INNOVATION

In his controversial book *The Closing of the American Mind: How Higher Education Has Failed Democracy and Impoverished the Souls of Today's Students*, Allan Bloom considered the marvelous gifts that technology has brought—and the common absence of understanding of this fact. Here he describes a combination of radio technology, music programming, and individualized listening:

> Picture a 13-year-old boy sitting in the living room of his family home doing this math assignment while wearing his Walkman headphones or watching MTV. He enjoys the liberties hard won over centuries by the alliance of philosophic genius and political heroism, consecrated by the blood of martyrs; he is provided with comfort and leisure by the most productive economy ever known to mankind; science has penetrated the secrets of nature in order to provide him with the marvelous, lifelike electronic sounds and image reproduction he is enjoying. And in what does progress culminate: A pubescent child whose body throbs with orgasmic rhythms; whose feelings are made articulate in hymns to the joys of onanism or the killing of parents;

whose ambition is to win fame and wealth in imitating the drag-queen who makes the music. In short, life is made into a nonstop, commercially, pre-packaged masturbational fantasy.[5]

Some observers dismissed Bloom's statements as grossly exaggerated and misstated. Others, noting the fanatic adherence of some rock music fans ("Rock Music Forever"), applauded him for articulating what had escaped the attention of others. Bloom went on to defend his position, implying that interpretation of his meaning may depend on the reader's value system and the pattern by which that value system has been shaped:

> This description may seem exaggerated, but only because some would prefer to regard it as such. The continuing exposure to rock music is a reality, not one confined to a particular class or type of child. [Rock music] is *the* youth culture and, as I have so often insisted, there is now no other countervailing nourishment for the spirit. . . .
>
> This phenomenon is both astounding and indigestible, and is hardly noticed, routine and habitual. But it is of historic proportions that a society's best young and their best energies should be so occupied. People of future civilizations will wonder at this and find it as incomprehensible as we do the caste system, witch burning, harems, cannibalism and gladiatorial combats. It may well be that a society's greatest madness seems normal to itself.[6]

It has been the habit of many artists on the edge of new modes of creativity to shock those who hold traditional values. Eccentricity at times has become popular, rather than remaining eccentric. It was so in the time of Socrates, Mozart, James Joyce, and the Beatles.

Case Study 5.4: Mandatory Advisories

As a community leader in the town where your radio station is situated, you have been asked to speak on the topic of mandatory advisory labels on records. You know that the audience that listens to you will be comprised of parents and teens, as well as businesses that advertise with you.

As you research the subject, you discover that many states have introduced legislation that would require records with "explicit" lyrics to be labeled with warnings. Typical of these warning labels would be bright yellow stickers reading:

> # WARNING: PARENTAL ADVISORY
> May contain explicit lyrics descriptive of or
> advocating one or more of the following:
> suicide—incest—bestiality—murder—
> sadomasochism—sexual activity in a violent
> context—morbid violence—illegal use
> of drugs or alcohol

At first examination, you are convinced that the advisory label is a good idea for the following reasons:

1. It addresses only the most explicit depictions of the most anti-social acts, nothing that you personally would want to run.
2. The nature of that which is being labeled could not be repeated in a newspaper or news broadcast in good taste. In fact, these lyrics, if written out, could not be mailed because of postal antiobscenity laws.
3. Actually, this is not much of an issue for you to discuss, because none of the lyrics could be aired legally anyway.
4. This is not an attempt to censor, as some have claimed. It is simply a matter of fully disclosing and warning of the content of what's inside. No material, no matter how explicit, would be excised from the albums themselves.
5. The labeling is an attempt to educate, inform, and enlighten as to what is in the lyrics, but it still allows families and parents the responsibility to raise their children based on informed consent, not ignorance.
6. Many questionable or potentially dangerous substances are labeled—a common practice in our society with such things as cigarettes, medicines, pesticides, and even food containing saccharin.
7. Why not put an advisory label on albums bearing highly questionable themes and song titles, such as "I Kill Children" by The Dead Kennedys; "Suicide Solution" by Ozzy Osbourne; and "Necrophiliac" by Slayer?[7]

The content of your speech is settled, then. Not only is the advisory labeling idea something that is within your own ethics and those of your station, but speaking out against such obviously distasteful stuff should bring nothing but praise from your community.

But then you read a newspaper column by a journalist who argues that such labeling violates a citizen's rights. This is no fanatic, no juvenile, no weirdo, but a well-respected intellectual. He makes the following points, which counter the ones you have already established:

1. Such labels are in fact censorship, since they throw into a "warning" category all artistic efforts that someone might consider questionable and want to label.
2. Who is to decide what material requires a label? The artist? The record company? The music store that sells it? The town council? Law enforcement officials? A government bureaucrat?
3. Most of the states' bills would fine and/or imprison the retail seller, even if he or she feels very differently about the material from the artist who produced the work.
4. "Label, just to be safe" might become the policy of many retail sellers responsible for labeling; "better to be safe than sorry." This all-encompassing attitude might sweep in albums that are really not offensive.
5. This focuses only on the lyrics, not the music. The pounding rhythms of rock music or even Ravel's crescendos in "Bolero" might be as prurient as any four-letter words in a lyric.
6. If labeling music lyrics seems appropriate, why not label TV programs, videos, concerts, and even commercials too? Why not label the "conventional violence" that is the main fare of much of today's entertainment media?[8] Labeling may mark the beginning of a whole crusade of muffling any kind of unconventional idea.

Which stand do you decide to take on mandatory advisories?

THE FAUSTIAN SCENARIO

How "dangerous" must an idea or an artistic expression be before it should be restricted, if there are to be restrictions? Can we trust the good judgment of social norms to recognize "evil" where it exists?

Evil is not a word that is commonly heard today outside religious contexts, but in past generations it was common in discussions of philosophy and ethics. For many centuries literature has used it and its struggle with "good" or "righteousness" as themes.

One of the more compelling and often-repeated themes of the good-evil syndrome in literature is the story of how man is attracted to do evil. It appears in the Genesis story of Eve tempted by the serpent, and in stories of attempts to gain superhuman wisdom, sometimes by treading into taboo areas or using black magic.

Soon after Johannes Gutenberg invented movable type in the fifteenth century, making printed stories popularly available, stories of humanized good and superhumanized evil appeared. Johann Faust, a character in medieval times, was first marketed in a crudely printed format by printer Johannes Spiess in 1587. The literary story of Faust described his powerfully appealing adventures in conjuring evil spirits and making deals with them in a blasphemous manner, turning the adventures into universal moral warnings. Soon after its translation from German into English, Christopher Marlowe was moved to compose the play *The Tragical History of Doctor Faustus* during the latter part of the sixteenth century. That drama, in turn, became a theme for folk culture puppet shows and other exhibits at communal festivals.

By the end of the eighteenth century German poet Johann Wolfgang von Goethe had written one of the greatest works of German literature, *Faust*. Its theme was familiar: In order to acquire power, riches, and glimpses of eternity,[9] Faust would make a pact with the evil one, Mephistopheles. Faust's obligation in return was his own soul. Mephistopheles would have the power to keep that eternal element of Faust and subject it to the fires of Hades or whatever else he should choose.

Two centuries ago, the lesson of the story was obvious to its hearers: Do not be like Faust, do not reach beyond mortality and covet the perspective of the gods and eternity, do not wish for ultramortal power and the pinnacle of wealth, worldly admiration, and eternal youth. This theme, found through traditionally accepted methods such as Scriptures or the inspiration of prophets and philosophers, was acceptable, if somewhat mundane. The idea continued to strike a responsive chord and remains a central theme in storytelling to this day.

This idea has fascinated composers—Wagner, Schumann, Berlioz, Gounod, Boito, and Mahler have all created scores of music or opera spun from Goethe's drama. Thomas Mann's epic novel *Doctor Faustus* treated the theme in the late 1940s, while in 1981 the motion picture *Mephisto* depicted an actor-director in Nazi Germany whose portrayal of Mephisto granted him fame and wealth reminiscent of Faust's.

The theme is found in American art as well, such as Stephen Vincent Benet's play *The Devil and Daniel Webster*, and Douglass Wallop's novel *The Year the Yankees Lost the Pennant*, which was made into the Broadway musical comedy *Damn Yankees*.

Where does all this lead us? The most recent manifestation of the Faust character is said to be in contemporary rock music artists. Superstar success among rock artists brings power, wealth, charisma, and the corruptive styles of irreverence, vulgarity, and pornography.

Observers of contemporary popular culture have noted that the highest incidence of devil worship and witchcraft occurs in the breweries of rock music. By some musicians' own admission (perhaps for the sake of gaining attention), the source of their inspiration is "the Devil." In 1963, Beatle John Lennon boasted that he received his inspiration "from Satan," and he later claimed himself more popular than Jesus Christ. Such statements prompted not only anger in the religious community for their blasphemous tone, but bewilderment as to why he should need to compare himself in such a way.

Mick Jagger of the Rolling Stones often credits the powers of darkness as the force behind his music. One of his greatest claims to fame is "Sympathy for the Devil," music that he boasts came directly from that source. Themes of and preoccupations with "Satan" and other expressions of fascination with the "Devil" and the macabre have come to dominate some artists' lyrics or themes in their stage presence.

Is this the influence of a "Mephistopheles"? Is the twentieth-century rock 'n' roll obsession with such themes

- an ironic turn back to medieval superstition?
- a purposeful use of a recognized literary theme?
- an actual Faustian trade-off with a real evil power?
- all pure coincidence?
- simply hype and attention-seeking?

Our reactions to and discussions of these five interpretations will clearly reflect our personal value systems. Such discussion could well prove to be enlightening.

MUSIC AND THE BROADCAST MEDIA

What is the role of the media—radio, records, TV, and especially music videos—in all of this?

First of all, the "reach" of radio is extensive and profound, so much so that it is difficult to overstate it. Radio is, as earlier promotions of the medium put it, "your constant companion." Not only do 99 percent of all households have radio (nearly all of them have more than one set), but 95 percent of all cars have radios. Each week it reaches 95 percent of all persons aged 12 and over, and it reaches nearly all teenagers during the course of a typical week. Listeners 12 and over spend an average of 20 hours each week with radio. Studies have shown that music, especially music heard via radio, is the single most dominant media influence in the lives of young adolescents and college-age adults.

Despite radio's heavy influence in American life, not all radio listening is to music. And even for people who are heavy music listeners, it is not certain what if any influence music has on them.

A second important factor is that radio has long been the popularizer of modern music. It is by virtue of airplay that music and musical artists gain their popularity and notoriety. Radio makes music part of today's cultural scene.

Shortly after radio first became a popular medium, in the 1930s, broadcasters battled with a music licenser, the American Society of Composers, Authors and Publishers (ASCAP), which demanded continually higher fees from stations for broadcasting music by the artists and composers it represented. Broadcasters, in turn, responded that the artists should be paying them—the stations—for playing their music, since the popularity brought about by broadcasting gave the music its value in the first place. Radio broadcasters felt so strongly about this that for a while they even refused to air licensed music. Soon, broadcasters created their own music licensing arrangements through an organization that later became known as Broadcast Music Incorporated (BMI).

Today, a large proportion of the revenues that go to the music industry and the musical artists, regardless of type of music, is derived from the licensing fees paid by radio (and television). This provides evidence that radio is in fact the lifeblood of popular music. But if this is the case, does radio bear part of the responsibility for whatever effect popular music may have?

It may be stretching matters to directly blame the radio stations that helped popularize Osbourne's "Suicide Solution," a song that prompted the suicide of a youth who had been obsessed with its ideas. On the other hand, is a radio station entirely without blame for any harmful results of airing music with themes of suicide, sexual promiscuity, bestiality, or macabre violence?

Clarifying Values in Broadcasting Music

The relationship between music and radio programming, the causal effects of antisocial themes in music lyrics, and the effects of the pounding rhythms of rock music may be too complicated to sort out in a straightforward values-clarification exercise. But in looking at the picture formed from such a situation, some approaches to the use of values can be articulated.

The Kantian categorical imperative (see Chapter 2) would have individuals adhere only to those values that they see as universally "true" or having some kind of "universal law." If your values tell you something is wrong, it's wrong, period; there can be no compromise and little, if any tolerance for other views. A radio program director who follows Kantian philosophy may strictly screen the music on the playlist.

Many individuals feel strongly about the "evil nature" of some of today's music and make little distinction between its appearance on recordings, over the radio, or as a music video. Lawmakers in Washington state passed a law making it illegal to sell music with "obscene lyrics" to minors, in much the same way that it is illegal to ban the sale of erotic printed materials, photographs, pictures, or motion pictures.

Senator Robert Byrd of West Virginia lashed out against the kinds of material commonly found in music videos: "Most rock musicians and actors in music videos emerge as sneering, antisocial, unkempt, undisciplined and arrogant punks. The central message of most of these music videos is clear: Human happiness and fulfillment are experienced by becoming a sociopath and rejecting all responsibility."

Senator Byrd went on to sound this ominous warning:

> If we in this nation continue to sow the images of murder, violence, drug abuse, sadism, arrogance, irreverence, blasphemy, perversion, pornography

and aberration before the eyes of millions of children, year after year and day after day, we should not be surprised if the foundations of our society rot away as if from leprosy.[10]

Is Senator Byrd right to feel so strongly? If rock music is so definitely evil, why is it not more widely recognized as such?

There are, of course, other perspectives, notably that the position Byrd typifies violates the important values of tolerance, freedom, and faith in others' ability to recognize truth or "evil."

One may take each of the other philosophical approaches to ethics discussed in Chapter 2 and apply them in like manner and estimate the results. Note that using different approaches often results in distinct philosophical "camps"—people who may seek wholly different solutions to the same circumstances.

NOTES

1. 18 U.S.C.A. §1464.
2. Richard Zoglin, "Shock Jock," *Time* (Nov. 30, 1992): 72–3.
3. Jon LaFayette, "A Stern Challenge," *Electronic Media* (Aug. 23, 1993), p. 4.
4. Rowan *v.* U.S. Post Office Department, 397 U.S. 728 (1970).
5. Allan Bloom, *The Closing of the American Mind: How Higher Education Has Failed Democracy and Impoverished the Souls of Today's Students* (New York: Simon and Schuster, 1987): 74–75.
6. Ibid.
7. These arguments in favor of labeling were put forth by Representative Ron Gamble of Pennsylvania, who introduced House Bill 1689 to place such advisory labels on a federal basis. His comments were printed in the Harrisburg, Pennsylvania, *Patriot-News*, Dec. 6, 1989.
8. These arguments against labeling were made by Tom Wicker, in the *New York Times*, in his column appearing Feb. 5, 1990, p. A19.
9. This all-encompassing moment was called the *Augenblick* in German, literally an "eyeblink"—a glimpse into eternity so profound, so sublime, that it surpassed all human experience and understanding. So overwhelming was the privilege of its acquisition that the tortures of hell were small punishment, indeed, in comparison.
10. Senator Robert Byrd, speech on the Senate floor, as reported in *Electronic Media* (Sept. 30, 1991): 8.

6

Television Programming and Values

Television programs with racy themes and shocking language are becoming increasingly common as we approach the twenty-first century. An older generation watches television and asks, "When did all this change? Where was I when the taboo suddenly became permissible?" When an older viewer exclaims in horror about the language and sexual themes that have come to dominate television today, a person from the younger generation simply shrugs and responds, "So?"

It is this difference in perception about expectations regarding values and ethics in program themes that has come to make any discussion of the situation so tricky and fraught with value snags. It is less a matter of the suddenness than the value shifts that have taken place. Whether those shifts have been "good" or "bad" is itself a value judgment that we perceive from our own value sets, stored up from years of experience, familial and religious influences, and impressions from the media themselves.

This chapter will trace some of these shifts and look at some of the programs that have posed questions in the ethics of TV programming.

Case Study 6.1: Success Versus Taste

The television program *Married . . . With Children* is being made at the studios where you are assigned as producer. In recent months, you have worked with your writers and creative staff to make this show something more than other mundane sitcoms—to allow it to be on the cutting edge of new ideas, not following conventional TV programming. Some critics see the show as "bad taste," but you always try not to go too far with never-before-handled themes and characters.

Now that the show has established itself and seems to be firmly in place, the writers push beyond the boundaries that the show itself has set up. You receive several scripts dealing with subjects not yet handled on *Married . . . With Children.*

One script deals with premenstrual syndrome (PMS). Humor on the subject is played out by the female lead character, Peg Bundy (played by Katy Segal). At one point, her husband Al wonders out loud whether PMS stands for "pummel men's scrotums." The network carrying the show, Fox Broadcasting Company (FBC), is usually more permissive than the other established networks, but it nonetheless orders this line cut out of the script. Your writers shrug and observe that this is the "cleaned-up" version of the script: "You should have seen it before we did our self-edits."

Do you defend the writers' right to retain the line, or do you submit to FBC's demands? After all, the network has the final say, in that it is ultimately responsible for what airs.

Your decision of whether to keep the line may hinge on how bad you think the line is. Does it go beyond the language itself? Are there insults or stereotypes implied by the line that undercut the dignity of some group? Is such humor to be allowed, on the assumption that the only people offended by it would be those without a sense of humor? Consider: Does your stand say anything about your philosophy, your value system, your view of the world?

But this is not the only problematic script. Others that have been called into question contain the following scenarios:

- Three of the female characters in the show go on a weekend fishing trip, and all have their menstrual periods at that time. The plot then goes on to develop humor, a story line, and emotional responses from this idea.
- In a Christmastime show, Santa Claus falls from a ledge, lands on his head, and dies in the Bundys' backyard.

- The teenage Bundys, Bud and Kelly, commiserate over their hatred of their parents. Their mother, Peg, appears to be pregnant. Kelly tells Bud, "I hate Mom! I mean, you can't blame Dad—he's just a stupid animal, but Mom knew what she was doing." In the meantime, Al, who is thinking of leaving Peg, is sitting at a bar ogling a nude dancer in front of him.
- Al charges men a fee for watching his daughter Kelly dance seductively for them. Bud develops his talents as a peeping Tom on the woman next door.

Generally, the show uses traditional family relationships as a source of humor, ridicules Al's sexual performance, and often engages in exercises of voyeurism. The one thing the Bundy family members have in common is their shared enjoyment of toilet and homosexual jokes.

The writers concede that their efforts are "to amuse and offend." The formula of using humor and staying as much as possible outside the traditional bounds of propriety seems to work. Like a pungent seasoning used in cooking, you can never be sure how much "offensiveness" will add the proper amount of spice and how much will overpower the whole dish. The writers continually explore combinations. Usually, the offensiveness seems to work well in a market that has become bored with the traditional and mundane.

By the end of its second year, *Married . . . With Children* had become a "flashpoint for the fall of standards on commercial television."[1] Yet in only a few years the show also became one of the most popular situation comedies. In rerun competition against other strip programs,[2] it is number one among adults 18 to 34. Using popularity as the sole value criterion, success is hard to argue with—unless you are of the opinion that there is a dangerous corrosive decline in social morals generally. In popular culture the taste of the masses—what critics term "slobcom"—becomes the norm and perpetuates both itself and themes that were at one time inappropriate on television.

Married . . . With Children was not the first situation comedy containing biting satire in the themes or language, and certainly it is not alone today. Many observers hold that most sitcoms on the air today use this element of social satire. Derisive humor and showing unpleasant realities have become standard practice.

Case Study 6.2: Applying Network Standards and Practices

As standards and practices chief for a TV network, you are told by the producers of the program that an episode of *L.A. Law,* which your network carries, may cause a public outcry. In the script for the episode a divorce lawyer refers to incriminating pictures of a couple engaged in a sexual act as "commonly described by a two-digit number." The language seems innocent enough, and only the sexually sophisticated viewer may even understand the reference to mutual oral sex. You decide to allow the reference to remain in the script.

Since programming on your network during prime time has not traditionally been pushing the boundaries of impropriety, you brace yourself for the airing of the episode and the wave of public protest that is sure to arise at the suggestive language.

But as it turns out, there are minimal complaints from the audience.

The question here is: Should you take this as a signal to allow more latitude with sexual suggestions in future episodes? Audience guidance in this "marketplace of ideas" seems to be doing little to discourage such double entendres in future scripts.

Despite the fact that you are of an older, more passive generation and your own values contradict pushing the boundaries of good taste and subtle references, do you do away with some of the network's older standards and practices policies? What role does your own value system play in your decision-making as trends move away from your values?

NETWORK STANDARDS AND PRACTICES: INTERNAL ETHICAL CODES

Each of the "big three" networks—ABC, CBS and NBC—once had, as part of its empire, a substantial set of codes known as *standards and practices* (or S&Ps for short). These were the internal "rules" by which the network determined what programming themes and language were acceptable.

These S&Ps received a big boost early in TV history, in 1959, after the infamous "quiz scandals." They were applied by network people who called themselves "monitors" but whom many regarded as "censors." These monitors applied such standards as the prohibition of hiding commercial advertisements within the program content (a practice that is now common in movies).[3]

Seldom did anyone contest the restrictions on nudity on network TV, or on the use of *goddamn,* or on the presentation of erotic sadomasochism, or on showing gay men together in bed. Some of the more troublesome and time-consuming network S&Ps were those governing advertising. It seems there were always advertisers who made questionable claims or used unacceptable techniques. (In November 1986, the S&Ps handbook of Capital Cities/ABC devoted only 21 pages to *program standards* but 99 pages to *advertising standards and guidelines.*) It wasn't always easy to have the S&Ps address all matters of concern.

Programming standards, for a time, seemed to take care of themselves. S&Ps were good business: They kept the government off the broadcasters' backs, since the broadcasters were regulating themselves, and they kept advertisers with questionable practices at bay, since the nets could point to S&Ps as the ultimate authority, like officiators in a ballgame.

Later, however, writers began to have trouble with the lines that S&P monitors drew. In one episode of NBC's *St. Elsewhere* the creators attempted to discuss the five most common methods of birth control. "They negotiated it down to three," the show's producer later said, noting that the capriciousness of the system got to him. A producer for a CBS show was persuaded to cut the number of gang rapists in an episode from seven to four. He wondered out loud why four was better than seven.[4]

When dramatic changes were made in S&Ps departments, it may have been partly a matter of producers' anger over capricious rules, but they seemed most strikingly brought about by financial concerns. As economic winds blew against network doors and their halls grew financially cold, more economic firewood was thrown in to keep the fires burning. Soon the ornamental furniture of standards and practices, now thought to be dispensable, was tossed on to keep the profits and dividends fired up. Since this happened at a time when the general tone of social morality and traditional ethics seemed to be relaxing, public reaction was minimal.

The three traditional networks went from S&Ps staffs of 30 to 50 each, to 10 or 15, and then to one network having a bare-bones staff of three or four. Recently, staffing has gone back up somewhat from there. Even now, much of S&Ps work has to do with monitoring standards in commercials; programming is largely ignored. Network programming has a new freedom, and with it, viewers find:

- The 1993 fall season began with the controversial series, *NYPD Blue*. Critics noted that it contained a hail of four-letter words and a bedroom scene that briefly included bare backsides and bared breasts. The series invoked the wrath of conservative groups who protested to the network, ABC, as well as advertisers and the FCC.
- Intimate conversations about orgasms and impotence on *thirtysomething*.
- Also on *thirtysomething*, the character Hope is seen taking her tank top off, revealing first her bare back, then part of the side of one breast. (Later, postproduction added a shadow over the side of the breast.)
- An entire episode of *Roseanne* concerned the title character's flatulence; another, her "boob reduction" surgery.
- Becky, the daughter in *Roseanne*, asks for birth control pills, to which Mom agrees because she dislikes the boyfriend and feels it important not to reproduce this guy.
- On *China Beach* a recurring character has been a likable prostitute.
- With a high percentage of teenagers among its viewers, *Beverly Hills 90210* seems to have a profound influence on young viewers, particularly its character Brenda. Shannen Doherty, who portrays Brenda, recently expressed concern about an episode in which her character loses her virginity. "I worried about how the audience would take it," she said. "I still believe there are virgins in this world—girls who want to say no. From now on they can look at my character and say, 'Wow, she's doing it, why can't we?'"[5]
- Viewers were assured that the characters on *Roc* were not suffering from "homophobia" in an episode when a family member brings his male lover home to meet the family. With rounds of laughs and guffaws, the script immunized the viewer against the usual clichés about homosexuals. Finally, a gay marriage is performed in the home. Following a kind of seasonal theme, this *Roc* plot is typical of many programs, both dramas and sitcoms, in which writers have worked with the gay community

to align storylines with the politically correct agenda of doing away with "homophobia."

- *Murphy Brown* and *Designing Women* are among programs that have taken advantage of the current absence of restraints on use of the words *penis* and *penis envy* in comic dialogue, coupling the word with references to the "little jackhammer."
- The NBC miniseries *Favorite Son* caused shock waves when it dealt with the subject of sexual bondage. In one scene a female character in bikini underclothes urges her lover to tie her to the bed.
- An episode of *Hill Street Blues* finds a murder scene where close to the victim is his pet sheep, his secret "paramour," with strong hints of bestiality.
- The writers of *St. Elsewhere* attempted to name a character "Connie Lingus." The NBC monitors renamed her simply "Constance."

It seems reasonable to assume that network S&Ps have been affected by the R-rated movies allowed on nonbroadcast cable and the different standards viewers see on rented videos. It was in these media that the looser trends were first seen, and the distinction between them and broadcast TV has become cloudy in the minds of many viewers.

According to one network vice-president over S&Ps, Rosalyn Weinman, "We allow a certain level of sexuality on the air not because we are competing with cable. It's very clear to me as a sociologist that we're not living in the time of Lucy and Desi."[6] Weinman then goes on to say that programming today reflects the more open attitudes about sex prevalent in the country that attitudinal surveys have revealed. In other words, television is a reflection of societal values more than a causal agent in creating them, she believes.

Case Study 6.3: "Those" Movies on Our Station?

Now as a program director of a local TV station, you are responsible for the purchasing of syndicated programs, including movie packages. Years ago, you are aware, before the era of movie video rentals, there was a great rivalry between the motion picture and television industries, and Hollywood deliberately began making movies that it felt could not be played on television, the more family oriented medium. Obscene language, graphic violence, sexual themes, and nudity became staples of most movies—along with the accompanying "R" rating. For many years, Hollywood's strategy worked— either those movies were not run on TV, or they were heavily edited for TV.

Now motion picture syndicators offer pictures that, not long ago, few people would ever have dreamed could be shown on television. Among the movies you, the program director, are being offered by a syndicator is *The Texas Chainsaw Massacre*. The syndicator guarantees you that the movie has been "edited for television." In previewing the film, you still find violence that seems excessive and gratuitous. Whoever edited the movie for television regarded it as acceptable to show blood oozing out of an eye or an ear and imply that a person is being sawed, but as unacceptable to show a limb being sawed off. To the editor, this distinction made sense, but it makes less sense to you. While you understand why the line was drawn there, you disagree with it, or perhaps even with the film's basic premise about the use of violence.

Other movies in the package have other kinds of problems. Some have plots that involve sexual liaisons, and when they are edited for TV, the storylines often simply don't make sense. Whether one's value system is liberal or conservative, the editing of these films for TV seems to be an injustice. Either it violates the creator's expression, or the movie doesn't fit comfortably into the different medium of television.

Your dilemma: Do you buy the films and air them at the risk of offending part of the viewing audience for their explicitness and offending perhaps another part because the films have been edited or dubbed beyond comprehensibility?

There is a positive side to the problem to consider as well. Experience has shown that usually these kinds of movie packages attract high ratings. Airing them would allow your station to get good advertising rates during their airing. To what extent do higher ratings, more money, and the profit incentive play a role in a decision-making process that also involves value judgments? Does airing programs involving violence or sexual themes constitute pandering, or is it an honest attempt to outdo the competition? To what extent do you cater to the lowest common denominator in programming to attract a larger audience?

THE PROBLEM OF VIOLENCE IN TV PROGRAMMING

Perhaps the oldest and most shopworn criticism of popular culture is that of its *violence*. Violence was of concern to parents in the era of the dime novel, and again in the genre of gangster movies and shoot-'em-up Westerns during the 1930s. Some of the first 1950s television programs carried the theme of solving conflicts by force and violence, although by today's standards, the violence involved seems bland indeed.

By the late 1960s, bolder themes and more graphic depictions became the subjects of study by government-funded researchers. In 1969 the surgeon general issued a comprehensive report that sounded a warning about the association between violence on television and the behavior of adolescents. Investigating Senate committees warned network chiefs that unless they cleaned up their programming, there would be legislative measures controlling programming. The networks responded, as did the FCC.

But such caution seemed to be transient. After creating a schism and promoting a "family viewing hour" in the time period before 9 P.M. (Eastern time), the networks allowed even more violence after 9 P.M. Violence in movies became more graphic, and that violence trickled into television as the movies were aired.

Pay cable, running R-rated movies with no restrictions or editing for television, began to change viewers' perception of what might appear on the TV screen.

Soon movies that had been intended to be watched only by restricted audiences in movie theaters came into the home, where people of all ages could watch them.

Consumer concern mounted. Groups such as the National Coalition on Television Violence sought to educate consumers and close the "gap between what research has found out and what the public knows."[7] This group is a coalition of researchers, physicians, psychiatrists, clergy, and lobbyists/activists. Its newsletter typically carries reports on the most violent movies, TV shows, cartoons, and toys, and news about the relationship between crime and media violence.

The effects of media violence are perhaps the most researched subject in the social sciences today. A review of the prolific and rich literature and even the major theories is not possible here. Suffice it to say that showing violence, especially on television and especially in large measures or in a gratuitous fashion, is an ethical question of immense proportions that is constantly addressed in the media.

The S&Ps policy regarding violence, as articulated by Capital Cities/ABC's guidelines, indicates an attempt to address the ethical problem without undue restriction of creative or First Amendment rights:

> The use of violence for sake of violence is prohibited. While a storyline or plot development may call for the use of force, the amount and manner of portrayal must be commensurate with a standard of reasonableness, with due regard for the principle that violence, or the use of force, as an appropriate means to an end, is not to be emulated. Additionally, while any act may be emulated, extreme caution must be observed in avoiding the portrayal of specific, detailed techniques involved in the use of weapons, the commission of crimes, and avoidance of detection.[8]

This passage reflects the following major ethical guidelines about televised violence:

- The violence needed to *realistically* portray character is distinguished from violence for violence's sake.
- The amount and manner of a portrayal must meet a standard of *reasonableness*.
- Violence should be presented as an *appropriate* means to the end it serves.
- Techniques of violence that would *encourage* criminal emulation are to be avoided.

Note that the italicized words here all imply some kind of subjective judgment that rests upon a person's ethical values. The various network monitors who make judgments as to what is reasonable, appropriate, and so on, are naturally going to differ in their judgment calls—perhaps even monitors within Capital Cities/ABC itself. And monitors will come to different conclusions as younger judges with different value sets come to assess programming content.

The split typified here among network monitors also represents the deep chasm in the research community. Noted researchers such as George Gerbner of the Annenberg School of

Communication at the University of Pennsylvania, have injected their own value systems into their work, concluding that the correlations that they have discovered between media violence and human behavior "cultivate" "threats to human dignity and the social order."[9] Others, concerned that true scientific research be objective and not clouded by individuals' personal ethics, disregard value-laden studies.

Here is a subject of intense and never-ending debate. Once again, it points not only to issues of media ethics but to the agenda behind much academic research. One may ask just what motivates academic researchers to examine so many facets of violence in the media? Is it wrong to undertake research out of concern for factors that affect human dignity and social order? What if your findings conclude something counter to your ethical perspective? Is *intolerance* of violence or any subject that one deems dangerous to human dignity and social order *unethical*, since "tolerance" is usually regarded as a *virtue* in value systems? Are there times when making a gesture that shows media messages and techniques that violate human dignity is more important than tolerating another's right of expression? In a society that has come to give paramount importance to the virtues of free expression, especially among the creative community working in the media, one may give great pause in answering these questions.

While the implications of these questions may go well beyond the agenda of a media, broadcast, or telecommunication ethics course, they are nevertheless vital in considering issues that have a bearing on ethics in the media.

Case Study 6.4: Should Stereotypes Be Censored?

As a writer for a television crime/action series, you have introduced a new character—a typical mafia crime boss with an Italian name. Language in the script not only is "colorful" but uses references to Italian-Americans that some consider to be "racial slurs." One of the heavies, a villainous character, is portrayed unflatteringly as a homosexual. His vicious and brutal acts are implied to be connected to his sexual orientation. The script also contains a heavy amount of violence, but you feel it is justified since the world of underground organized crime is admittedly full of such acts.

The program producer has a few misgivings about some parts of your script, but overall he says it is "powerful" and wants to proceed with production. In the meantime, several groups, including Italian-Americans, Queer Nation, and the National Coalition on Television Violence all warn that "unfortunate stereotypes and images . . . must be changed . . . or face the wrath and boycotts" of these groups.

As a writer, you feel that artists at the cutting edge of new ideas and progressive concepts are often subjected to negative public sentiment. You feel yourself to be at such a horizon. You understand, too, that unless you "compromise" your artistic work, it will not be used. Your work simply will not appear, and you will gain no recognition as an artist. Do you hold to your ideals and fight to keep your characters in the script, or do you accede to the demands of the producer and the watchdog groups? Consider the issues introduced above (program themes, violence, and the like) and the problem of freedom of expression in a medium whose standards are not currently in keeping with what you propose. Can you defend the position even if you are not sympathetic to it? How important is the free expression of ideas? How vital is it to be part of the "politically correct" scene?

THE ORIGIN OF PROGRAM THEMES: DEFINING THE CREATIVE COMMUNITY

Who are the writers and creators of today's programming fare? Do they typify the viewers who see their creations? Do they reflect social values, or do they project their own values, hoping to gain some kind of social approval for them?

Such questions have been posed by researchers, including Stanley Rothman and Robert and Linda Lichter. They have written previously of *The Media Elite*[10] and have further developed their ideas in a newer work, *Watching America: What Television Tells Us About Our Lives*.[11] Both studies regard the creative community that develops the themes, storylines, and language of what millions see every day and every night on television as the elite who don't reflect the real values of Americans.

In the earlier study, the researchers conducted interviews with 104 of "Hollywood's most influential television writers, producers and executives, as part of a larger study of elite groups." They constructed the sample from a list of individuals whose reputations were identified by a number of "insiders" in the field. The survey discovered the following:

- 99 percent of the creators were white (compared with 84 percent of the U.S. population).
- 98 percent were male (compared with 49 percent of the population).
- 63 percent had an annual income of over $200,000; 25 percent of over half a million (the average U.S. income is about $24,000).
- 44 percent listed as their religion "none" (compared with 4 percent of Americans who claim no religious affiliation).
- 7 percent were regular churchgoers (compared with 47 percent nationally).
- 66 percent felt that TV should be used to promote social reform.
- 70 percent felt that there was *not* too much sex on TV.
- 41 percent felt that there was *not* too much violence on TV.
- 97 percent support abortion rights (compared with 59 percent nationally).
- 20 percent feel that homosexuality is wrong (compared with 76 percent nationally).
- 49 percent feel that adultery is wrong (compared with 85 percent nationally).

This profile, the researchers point out, is hardly typical of the values of middle America. And since TV viewers tend to adopt the values they see in a cumulative manner, the perceptions of life of this "elite" group are the values that are coming to the forefront of American society today.

Moreover, if this idea is coupled with Gerbner's "cultivation" idea, there is a real possibility that the fictitious ideas portrayed on television come to be regarded as reality by TV viewers, especially by those who view TV heavily.

Since many of the ideas on attitudes portrayed on television come to define reality and shape our own values, *the setting of ethics in the creation of television programming has enormous implications.* Orwellian control of thinking by such instruments of mass communication may no longer be just a fantasy in some writer's imagination.

PROGRAMMING SCHEDULING—
DONE WITH AN EYE TO ETHICS
Case Study 6.5: The Programming Scheduler

Part of the job of program director is to strategically place TV programs so that they will effectively deflate the competition and so that the programming lineup is complementary and effective. Another part of the job is to determine what the demographics are during the time period when a program is offered. As the program director of a major-market TV station, you are to decide whether a syndicated package of horror shows should be telecast early or late on Saturday evenings. You understand that putting it later at night will pit it against *Saturday Night Live,* for which there is a large audience. That competition would hurt the ratings of your horror show and lessen the value of the advertising, from which you would expect the station to profit.

The promotions for the horror show tell you: "The nature of horror is to delve into as many areas that are either shocking or break boundaries, and the nature of TV is to have boundaries. . . . Use caution in scheduling this program."[12]

Colleagues in the profession have warned you that you had better be prepared for some viewer complaints. The themes and the depictions of violence are awfully graphic. Ethics is part of the issue, keeping the less savory stuff as far as possible from younger viewers who might happen to see it. It seems that you would be safer placing the programs in the late-evening time slot, but there would be less financial advantage.

Consider: How do you justify the later time slot to management, which is working in every conceivable way to maximize profits? Should the program be used at all? These ethical considerations seem to be pitted against efficiently making money.

Some thinking in programming executive circles implies that if a program has themes, language, or scenes that might be offensive to a family viewing audience, then it should be placed in a later time slot. Networks have done this when they have come under criticism for excessive violence. A "family viewing hour" was defined where there was little, if any, sex and violence before nine o'clock. Some critics claim that this resulted in *more* such fare being introduced after the family viewing hour ended.

In 1978, when a U.S. Supreme Court case examined the issue of "indecent language" in radio, the implication was made that if the program had been aired at night, when the audience had consisted of fewer children, such language may have been tolerable.[13] Would the same hold true for television?

The FCC eventually indicated that there might be a "safe harbor," wherein materials previously deemed "indecent" would be allowed. At first, this "harbor" was set at from 10 P.M. until 6 A.M.; then, after numerous complaints that radio programming was getting worse, it was moved back to from midnight to 6 A.M. More recently, the Commission has imposed a 24-hour ban on indecency on both radio and broadcast television (over-the-air TV). Battles continue to rage over whether a 24-hour ban on material thought to be indecent violates the First Amendment.

Nevertheless, many programmers do put more questionable material in later evening hours. For many years, the material on the *Tonight* show has been of a more adult nature than much of what comes on earlier in the evening. Ditto for *Saturday Night Live* and *David Letterman*. Some provocative talk shows, as well as double entendre programs such as *Studs,* have found their niche audience at later evening hours.[14]

Case Study 6.6: Programs That Attract Attention

A new talk-show program is getting widespread attention for its outrageous guests. For example, one show is to feature punk rocker G. G. Allin. In his act, he defecates onstage, eats it, and throws it at the audience. He breaks glass and rolls around in it; he attacks people. Most people might consider such stuff repulsive, but they will watch it just the same. As program director, do you acquire it for your station?[15]

Another new package of programs that feature stand-up comics with mature humor is being made available as well. It is featured as a series of programs of "irreverence and insanity with the world's most recognized stand-up comics.... Nothing is sacred anymore!!" You are assured that this series is "HOT!!" and that you can be sure that viewers will watch your station just to be informed of the latest jokes about Pee-wee Herman, among others. It's sure to help your ratings and positively affect the ratings of programs that come before and after it.

Consider: As program director, do you go for these two programs? Are there any ethics issues involved here? If so, what are they? Will basing your decision on them affect your performance as a member of a team dedicated to putting your station ahead of its competition?

Many of the case studies in this chapter deal with the same basic problem: the ethics of a program's daring theme, language, and so on, versus the ability to maximize profits from that program. It should be obvious by now that there is no magic boundary upon which the parties involved in making such judgments can agree.

However, saying decisions should be made on a case-by-case basis implies that we accept the notion of *situational ethics*, where the values demonstrated depend on circumstances. In most respects, this is quite the opposite of the Kantian ethical philosophy of the categorical imperative, where truth is truth regardless of where you find it or what the circumstances are.

POPULAR CULTURE: LETTING THE MARKETPLACE DECIDE

The idea of the categorical imperative (see Chapter 2) evokes another issue connected with media ethics and television programming. Our media have created around us a *popular culture*. In this culture media content gravitates toward what its beholders consider the most attractive, or toward that which attracts the most attention. We vote by our viewing habits. By virtue of watching a specific program on a certain channel, we "cast our vote" for that program in a kind of "cultural democracy." Television programming success seems to be easily determined in a setting where the highest ratings dictate what endures. With such an approach, we assume that the collective judgment of television viewers is the best way of judging what is worth keeping, as in a political election. In a more contemporary and economic expression, "Let the marketplace decide."

There are problems with this approach, too, problems that address themselves to both a conservative and a liberal outlook.

First, if popularity is the key to determining enduring success, where is there room for the new ideas, the creative, the untried, the nontraditional? Just how do new artists come to be accepted? And if there is room for acceptance of new ideas, how is the culture to differentiate between garbage of no value and ideas that are ingenious, perhaps even great, but that go unnoticed by the masses?

Second, there certainly must be someone who makes the new product. Who is to guide us or tell us which new products are great and which are garbage? Who is the critic or expert who dares to distinguish between popular garbage and unpopular greatness? Do we entrust a kind of culture elitist to make this distinction? If so, would this not violate the rules of popular culture?

Third, how do we assess the values of programs that do little to enlighten or ennoble the human spirit but that attract large masses because of their temporarily exciting nature—programs full of car chases, shoot 'em up, and titillating sex scenes? Have we lost our capacity to distinguish between the titillating and the profound?

Fourth, if nonrepresentative groups of creative elites are imposing their values on us through TV programming, as Lichter et al. claim, where is there room for real choice by the middle American viewer? It has been argued that the programs shown on television today offer little for the person interested in a whole array of other ideas and values—the classics, the sciences, and simply some important how-to's for today's living. While this may be less true today because of the numerous cable channels, it still remains a problem in our popular culture.

Fifth, if the television industry is primarily a business and only secondarily an art form of entertainment, the "marketplace" is whatever brings higher profits, not necessarily that which appeals to important ethical values.

Sixth, are viewers, consumers, and the marketplace really best represented by the usual ratings measurements? Is something more simple than viewing habits involved? If a group has concerns, for example, about the values being displayed on television, how are the concerns of such a group to be voiced, and through what means? Viewers are generally reluctant to write letters of protest to stations, networks, the FCC, or the government, as I have elsewhere noted: "Most media consumers do not lobby for laws restraining the media. Groups that do represent the media are often regarded as strident, radical troublemakers: the Ralph Naders, the Donald Wildmons, the Reed Irvines of this popular culture. Where is the provision for moderates in this voice of the marketplace? Or will the moderates remain silent?"[16]

VIEWERS' OPTIONS FOR EXPRESSING VALUE PREFERENCES

Students of research methodology know that if a survey is to be considered valid, it must follow careful objective procedures, such as being free from bias, having a representative sample, and the like. Validity is more strongly established when more than one means of gathering data is used. If a qualitative as well as a quantitative measure were used to ascertain viewer preferences, ratings for television viewing would be enhanced. Rating services will claim that this is already being done because they look at demographic figures and sample responses about familiarity with shows or their characters. Yet a gap remains in examining viewers' reactions to values displayed in programs—beyond, of course, whether viewers turn off the set or leave it on, certainly a crude means of examining where the fine lines of acceptable and unacceptable values may be drawn.

What are the optional means that viewers have to voice their reactions to marketplace decisions, particularly reactions that are not in keeping with the norms coming from the "creative community"?

Some viewers have objected so strongly to how some values are portrayed, characterized or ridiculed that they have set up their own monitoring groups. The American Family Association (AFA), for example, makes a practice of watching for movies, magazines, and television programs that may violate the values of the traditional Christian family. Each month, its *AFA Journal* cites outrageous episodes on TV and identifies the programs' advertisers and their addresses. The idea is that readers are to write those products' companies, expressing concern that they are condoning objectionable values by economically supporting these violating programs through advertising. Sometimes the AFA also names what it considers prosocial programs, suggesting that readers give support or pats on the back to those advertisers, also identified.

It may be that such value-oriented consumer groups will become more popular as viewers become more conscious of how their different values can be fed back to the media.

Some stations and networks are aware of such grassroots movements and are devising public relations efforts to assure these groups that they are sensitive to those groups' ethical concerns.

Writers, producers, creators, and programmers cannot continue to work in the 1990s without becoming aware of the ethical dilemmas involved in their work. This chapter has been designed to assist the reader in identifying what those challenges and dilemmas might be.

NOTES

1. Steven Beschloss, "Making the Rules in Prime Time," *Channels* (May 7, 1990): 23.
2. A "strip program" is a program, often a rerun from the original series, run on a regular daily basis—stripped across the schedule. This *Married . . . With Children* strip consists of reruns from the earlier airing by FBC. The other strip programs against which the program successfully ran were *Oprah Winfrey, The Cosby Show, Entertainment Tonight, A Current Affair, Jeopardy, Wheel of Fortune, Love Connection, Donahue,* and *Hard Copy.* Source: NSS, 1991-92 STD through 3/1/92, as cited in *Electronic Media* (Mar. 16, 1992): 18–19.
3. An excellent discussion of this is found in Muriel Cantor's *Prime Time Television: Content and Control* (Thousand Oaks, Ca.: Sage Publications, 1980).
4. Cited in L. J. Davis, "Looser, Yes, But Still the Deans of Discipline," *Channels* (Jul.–Aug. 1987): 34.
5. Shannen Doherty quoted in Associated Press, Aug. 22, 1991.
6. Beschloss, "Making the Rules," 25.
7. Joseph Strayhorn, M.D. "Strategies for Reducing Exposure to Violent Movies: Questions Answered and Unanswered," *NCTV News* 12:3–5 (Jun.–Aug. 1991): 5.
8. Capital Cities/ABC, *Program Standards* (1986): 21.
9. George Gerbner, "Symbolic Function of Violence and Terror," published as part of the series *Terrorism and the News Media: Research Project*, Robert G. Picard (ed.), (Columbia, S.C.: Association for Education in Journalism and Mass Communication, 1986).
10. S. Robert Lichter, Stanley Rothman, and Linda S. Lichter, *The Media Elite* (Bethesda, Md.: Adler and Adler, 1986).

11. S. Robert Lichter, Linda S. Lichter, and Stanley Rothman, *Watching America: What Television Tells Us About Our Lives* (Englewood Cliffs, N.J.: Prentice-Hall, 1991).

12. Quoted in "Scary Shows," *Electronic Media* (Oct. 28, 1991): 1, 32.

13. FCC *v.* Pacifica Foundation, 438 U.S. 726, 3 *Med.L.Rptr.* 2553 (1978).

14. See *Electronic Media* (Dec. 30, 1991): 1; also *Electronic Media* (Aug. 19, 1991): 4.

15. Allin was actually booked for the *Morton Downey Jr. Show,* but he could not appear for the taping: "he was jailed the day before for inflicting several thousand dollars worth of damage upon the hotel room the show had provided." *Channels* (Oct. 1988): 62.

16. Val Limburg, "The Decline of Broadcast Ethics: U.S. *v.* NAB," *Journal of Mass Media Ethics* 4:2 (1989): 223.

7

Broadcast News Ethics

Case Study 7.1: The Early Cost of News

In the early years of broadcast news, much of radio did not seem very serious in its journalistic efforts. For the first decade, most radio "news announcers" simply read the news from accounts of other reporters rather than go out on the street for stories. That was the situation in the mid-1930s, when newspaper publishers persuaded the news wire services to constrain radio:

- Radio was not allowed to air the news until after it had appeared in print in a newspaper.
- There could be no more than ten minutes of news per day.
- News had to be free from commercial support.

Some publishers even pushed for Congress to legislate restrictions that barred radio from carrying news, since its ability to deliver news so much faster than print media could be a financial disaster for the great publishing empires. For some, it would seem an irony that in the value conflict between economics and news, journalists would subordinate the First Amendment and grant a higher priority to the profit incentive under such conditions.

Should there be control of competition? The real threat to publishers was the very existence of competition, in which the rival could deliver news faster in a setting where speed ("the scoop") was the key element of success. The press can talk all it wants about First Amendment rights, but if the competition outdoes you, you must close down, and there goes the voice of the press—at least in its traditional print form. The reality of the threat is evidenced by the fact that some publishers met the challenge by acquiring the licenses for many early radio stations: "If you can't beat 'em, buy out the competition!"

Should there be no control of competition? To what extent do the philosophy and value system of a free press mandate that the government make no laws abridging a free press, even at the risk of the very continuance of a free press? Does confinement of the news to a single medium restrict the free flow of information? Must truth be allowed to pass unobstructed through as many avenues as possible in order to be recognized and embraced in a free and open marketplace of ideas? Was there a value conflict here—where publishers were pitting their economic interests against freedom of the press?

THE FIRST AMENDMENT AND THE FREE FLOW OF INFORMATION

In this historical case study and in other instances of clashes between economics and information flow, it becomes apparent that the issue is one of pragmatics versus idealism.

We could best discover truth, it was long thought, if we had access to all possible information. In a free and open encounter with falsehood, truth would win out. So did the poet John Milton articulate the view in his *Areopagitica* in the mid-seventeenth century. There he affirmed his deep belief in our inherent God-given ability to recognize truth, even when mixed with error. This notion of *the self-righting process* became a part of American colonial political thought that defined freedom as the right to know, to understand, and to reason. Without such rights, man is but an animal and not a real human being.

It was this thinking that, together with other ideas, shaped the First Amendment of the U.S. Constitution:

Congress shall make no law respecting an establishment of religion, or prohibiting the free exercise thereof; or abridging the freedom of speech, or of the press; or the right of the people peaceably to assemble, and to petition the Government for a redress of grievances.

Since this inception more than 200 years ago, journalists have fought to preserve the First Amendment and its liberty of the press. More courtroom battles may have ensued over this constitutional right than any other. Yet in the 1930s this philosophical freedom seemed an abstract ideal void of any reality if the press were not to be able to survive economically. If the press failed financially, there would be no press, so what did it matter that there was a First Amendment right for the press?

This is perhaps the most fundamental of all conflicts in the media: that of a free press and the free flow of information versus the profit incentive. This case study is a microcosm of many of the problems and dilemmas that exist today and have existed over many years in the media.

While this dilemma exists for both print and broadcast media, there are a number of episodes in the history of radio and television that fully bring to light this problem.

THE IDEALS OF EARLY BROADCAST NEWS: EDWARD R. MURROW

From London in the early 1940s, short-wave reports of World War II were dramatically relayed by Edward R. Murrow and carried over the Columbia Broadcasting System (CBS). It was part of the beginning of radio as a legitimate news medium. Murrow, whose striking voice captured the ears of a war-wary nation, became the electronic media's first recognized *broadcast journalist,* a combination of terms not easily assimilated by print reporters. It was during this wartime crisis that radio distinguished itself as a valuable, if not critical news medium.

CBS was learning that its ability to carry this vital news service also allowed it to make money. There seemed to be nothing wrong with serving two valuable functions at once.

Yet shortly after the war, sometime during the 1940s or early 1950s, radio news evolved from being primarily a service for the benefit of its listeners' enlightenment to being a commodity that could be sold. For the advertisers who sponsored or advertised during the news and for the listeners whose exposure to the news also exposed them to advertisements, there was mutual benefit, especially to the advertisers and to the business side of the radio industry.

In 1958, after radio had more and more made news a commodity, Murrow looked back at the "progress" of the previous few years:

So far as radio—that most satisfying and rewarding instrument—is concerned, the diagnosis of its difficulties is rather easy. And obviously I speak only of news and information. In order to progress it need only go backward. To the time when singing commercials were not allowed on news reports, when there was no middle commercial in a fifteen-minute news report; when radio was rather proud, alert and fast. I recently asked a network official: Why this great rash of five-minute news reports (including three commercials) on week ends? He replied: "Because that seems to be the only thing we can sell."[1]

Murrow, whose ideals were and still are greatly respected, went on to challenge the media to compete "not only in selling soap, cigarettes and automobiles, but in informing a troubled, apprehensive but receptive public."[2] He encouraged the large Wall Street corporations whose advertising dominated radio and television to offer some of their regularly scheduled time slots to discuss vital public issues.

When television came on the scene, Murrow was there, too, adapting his radio program *Hear It Now* to television as *See It Now*. His impact soon became obvious in television with such programs as *CBS Reports*. At this time a U.S. Senator from Wisconsin, Joseph McCarthy, was taking advantage of the nation's fear of Communism in the House Un-American Activities Committee, browbeating and using innuendo to accuse various public figures and citizens of being Communists. McCarthy's tactics became the subject of one of Murrow's *See It Now* programs. The program vividly revealed the nature of the techniques and threats the politician was making, proving to be his undoing.

Murrow showed how television could be a merciless revealer of personality and subtlety. It could reveal previously unexplored truths, at least to the designer or producer of the program. TV was clearly becoming a powerful instrument of news. But Murrow also could see the medium being misused by profiteers, and he warned of our inattention to TV's great potential:

This instrument can teach, it can illuminate; yes, and it can even inspire. But it can do so only to the extent that humans are determined to use it to those ends. Otherwise it is merely wires and lights in a box. There is a great and perhaps decisive battle to be fought against ignorance, intolerance and indifference. This weapon of television could be useful.[3]

At a time when the television business was defining its economic direction and what it was to become, Murrow reminded everyone of its more noble ideals.

One of Murrow's colleagues at CBS was a young producer, Fred W. Friendly. Friendly worked with Murrow on *CBS Reports* and was with him on TV's first live national network news program. After Murrow left CBS to head up the U.S. Information Agency in the Kennedy administration, Friendly became president of CBS News. There he carried on the Murrow tradition of battling the corporate executives for the journalistic ideals of television as an important news medium.

Case Study 7.2: A Friendly Reminder of TV's Values

In 1967 an important event highlighted the pragmatic versus idealist dilemma of network TV. It was a time when congressional hearings were being held on a war in faraway Indochina, or Vietnam. Although U.S. policy was being shaped by the hearings, they seemed unimportant to much of the public. Fred Friendly, seeing an important issue to which TV should give a public forum, sought live daytime coverage of the hearings.

The network executives, anxious not to show losses to shareholders, were concerned about advertising revenues that might be lost with sustained congressional coverage. Running regular programming, even reruns of *I Love Lucy*, would provide more revenue than congressional coverage would. As a matter of fact, Friendly figured that the special coverage would cost the network a quarter of a million dollars.

So reruns it was. "A system designed to respond to the stock market," he observed, "which in turn responds to ratings, was governed more by concern for growth and earnings than for news responsibility."[4] Rather than compromise his ideals concerning the priority of news values, Friendly resigned and left CBS.

That was nearly thirty years ago. Today, Friendly tries the ideals of journalists and media managers by staging "media hypotheticals." Here is his real-life case study: Would you do the same—leave a network and a high-paying position—because of your ideals, or would you remain part of the profit-oriented working team? Using Friendly's situation consider:

- the ideals of the potential of news for radio or television;
- the necessity of turning profits in order to maintain a viable medium capable of carrying the news;
- the fact that viewers would likely rather watch *Lucy* reruns than congressional hearings;
- the extent to which a news person, responsible for making news judgments and decisions, should be answerable to a business executive.

Historically, some presumptions have been made that the influence of radio and television is so powerful that there needs be control of them. This control has been manifested in the following policies of the Federal Communications Commission (FCC), the federal agency responsible for overseeing broadcasting.

- A station owner, licensee, or corporation is limited in the number of stations that may be operated under single ownership.
- A station owner must be of U.S. citizenship, without serious criminal record, and of sound financial reputation and ability.
- In issues of public controversy, stations have, in the past, been responsible for seeking out and presenting all sides of the issue to insure a balance—a fairness. This FCC policy became known as the *Fairness Doctrine*.
- Section 315 of the Communications Act mandates that stations must give political candidates "equal time."

Some of these policies have been modified in recent years, as the mood in Washington has shifted to deregulation.

The Fairness Doctrine was a government policy that affected broadcast news (and *only* broadcast news) and how a broadcast journalist must operate—in a word, to achieve "balance." While it was in effect, the Fairness Doctrine forced what was perceived to be balance by requiring all sides of an issue to be aired.[5]

Good journalists, it was believed, would naturally balance their stories anyway, since that was part of journalism ethics. The Code of Broadcast News Ethics of the Radio/Television News Directors Association states that a reporter's purpose is "to inform the public . . . in a manner that is accurate and comprehensive . . . [and that] shall override all other purposes."[6] Those who violated fairness standards deserved some kind of discipline, it was reasoned. So why should anyone object to the formalized doctrine?

The idea of Big Brother government watching over the shoulders of journalists, however, bothered many people, and not just reporters. You cannot legislate morality, it was argued, regardless of your good intentions. In 1967, broadcasters challenged the Fairness Doctrine in court and lost,[7] but they continued to fight it, reasoning that the government had no business stipulating what a journalist should or should not say, even if the intent was to ensure "fairness."

During the Reagan administration, however, the mood of government deregulation penetrated the FCC. In 1987, the FCC struck down the Fairness Doctrine and no longer enforced it.

Some news staffs continued to observe the Fairness Doctrine as part of good journalism, but even they were relieved that they no longer had to answer to the FCC for how they executed the policy. Other news reporters went ahead and covered stories in ways that reflected only a singular perspective.

Often it was public figures and public officials, including congressmen, who were affected by unbalanced coverage. It seems natural, then, that since 1987 Congress has moved to revive the Fairness Doctrine by legislation, introducing a law that would be part of the Communications Act. The bill met with presidential vetos by Reagan and Bush, but the threat of a legislated Fairness Doctrine remains; it is not a government-mandated policy at the time of this writing.

The doctrine's value in guiding broadcasters is a matter of debate. One may consider current issues as the media have unraveled them, whether there has been unfair (or at least unbalanced) coverage, and whether such coverage implores revival of the Fairness Doctrine.

Case Study 7.3: *60 Minutes* and the Alar Scare

On February 26, 1989, CBS's *60 Minutes* aired a story entitled "A is for Apple." The introduction by Ed Bradley contained a background visual of a red apple on which was superimposed a skull and crossbones. Bradley began: "The most potent cancer-causing agent in our food supply is a substance sprayed on apples to keep them on the trees longer and make them look better. That's the conclusion of a number of scientific experts, and who is most at risk? Children who may someday develop cancer from this one chemical called daminozide (Alar). Daminozide, which has been sprayed on apples for more than 20 years, breaks down into another chemical called UDMH."

It was estimated that 50 million viewers saw the segment and assumed, along with the producers of the program, that the claims the story quoted from a report of the National Resources Defense Council (NRDC) were true. The program caused a near-panic. Consumers and school lunchrooms alike stopped buying all apples, although most had no contact with daminozide or Alar. Within months, apple growers became bankrupt. Apple juice was dumped down the drain, and apple exports to other countries were halted. Meryl Streep, who co-founded an advocacy group called Mothers and Others for Pesticide Limits, pitched a booklet with a 900 phone number, from which NRDC ultimately gleaned over half a million dollars. As president of the Mountain States Legal Foundation, William Perry Pendley, noted, "Not since Orson Welles' Mercury Theater of the Air inadvertently panicked a nation with a 1938 Halloween night adaptation of H. G. Wells's *War of the Worlds* about aliens invading New Jersey has there been a broadcast which caused the American public to act in such an irrational manner."[8]

Much of the information proved later to be bogus. The danger from Alar was minimal; *60 Minutes* had greatly overstated it. Moreover, it was found, the information used on the program actually had come from "a high-powered public relations firm [that had] secretly crafted the Alar scare for the NRDC and released it to CBS and other media in a well-orchestrated publicity campaign" to raise funds.[9]

The issue here is not that advocacy points of view were aired. The issue is that a balance, revealing other points of view, was deliberately avoided. After threats of legal action and publicity by the consumer advocacy group Accuracy in Media (AIM), CBS agreed to air a follow-up program and scheduled it for May 14.

One of the plaintiffs in the threatened action against CBS was apple grower and attorney J. Jarrette Sandlin. Sandlin went to New York to be interviewed by the CBS producers. According to his account of the meeting, much information about the safety of Alar, its warning label and research statistics, were shown to the producers and reporters of *60 Minutes*. They had never seen it before. Nor did it appear on the follow-up program because, according to Sandlin, "it would have destroyed their whole story."[10]

CBS, according to those engaged in this issue, had a vested interest in keeping its original advocacy side of the story and in not trying to balance it subsequently, perhaps partly for legal reasons, or partly out of pride—not many people like to admit they were wrong.

Despite its tradition of Edward R. Murrow and of being the pathfinder of broadcast news ethics, CBS was violating the very practice considered good ethics in TV news: balance.

Many people who viewed the program may have received the impression that balance existed. The apple growers who were plaintiffs in the case claim that such impressions were part of the deception.

In this case study, consider the following:

- Should balance be required for all stories? Is there no room for "advocacy journalism"?
- Since many issues are complex, even scientifically complicated, to what extent should a reporter or producer rely on the expertise of someone else, especially if such briefers have a vested interest or hidden agenda?
- Should litigation (that is, threat of a lawsuit) be something that motivates "fair reporting"?
- With the demise of the Fairness Doctrine, what watchdog is there to keep the media honest and in line?

Perhaps after viewing a videotape of the *60 Minutes* program and its follow-up, discussion could ensue over the reporting techniques or the information and lack of information used in the program. Background information giving the other side of the story from CBS's version can be found in *Fear of Food* by Andrea Arnold.[11]

Often the area of conflict is not within the realm of journalism, but between the reporters and media owners. This may have been the situation with Fred Friendly's resignation (see Case Study 7.2). A more recent case demonstrates another conflict in which different interests within a news medium are pitted against each other.

Case Study 7.4: The Rose Bowl–Bound Football Team

A Rose Bowl–bound football team, the University of Washington Huskies, was the subject of two TV news reports by award-winning reporter Mark Sauter. Sauter's stories were not in keeping with the other, glowing reports of the champions, who were heroes in the eyes of many. His first report said the Huskies' players had the lowest graduating rate of any Pacific-10 Conference football team. The second story never got to the air. It disclosed that several of the players had active arrest warrants out for them. The charges ranged from DWI to assault. The story noted an apparent tendency among the players not to respond to warrants ordering them to appear in court.

The president of the television station usurped the reporter's notes, then conferred with the university president and the vice-president for university relations. After examining the reports, they claimed that the stories were calculated to embarrass the Huskies more than anything else. The second story never ran.

Should it have been run? Here are the issues:

1. Should a television station president have the final say about whether a news story should appear on a news program?
2. In the interests of airing all sides of the issue and letting the public find out the truth, should the football coach and players have been allowed to respond to the charges? The charges were now leaked by other media in a manner that was probably more damaging than airing the original story would have been.
3. Are there allegiances whose importance overrides the disclosure of claims in a news story? When, if ever, should information be held back? To what should one be most loyal?
4. Can management create a chilling atmosphere among reporters, causing them to fear covering certain stories or facts, knowing that they may be censored or be terminated?
5. Was the privacy of the football team members invaded by a press that was after them simply because of their fame and success? Would this have happened if the players had been in a losing season?
6. Should the station have played down subsequent stories about the "coverup" in an effort to avoid tarnishing its image of integrity?

In a practical way, the economics of news is reflected by *ratings.* Higher ratings mean more people watching, and advertising rates are higher, meaning more profit for the station. Those who are in television for business reasons may see the need to create news with an eye to boosting ratings. Often news reporting is accused of being sensationalized for the purpose of attracting viewers, rather than simply disclosing legitimate issues of public importance. The problem is, what constitutes "issues of public importance"?

Case Study 7.5: News Values Versus News Ratings

A fascination with the supernatural has been a recurring theme both in literature and in current news stories—even in the enlightened closing of the twentieth century.

In one spring period, satanic rituals were the subject of stories by two competing TV stations. This period just happened to be the "May sweeps," the time when ratings or viewership is measured. Helicopters from the two TV stations hovered over wooded areas, looking for "satanic burial grounds." Three weeks' worth of special reports on the subject were promoted and reported on the local newscasts, but the end result was that there were no bodies, no burial grounds, no shocking cult activity. Despite the absence of facts, however, the stories persisted until the last day of the rating period.

It worked. The two stations carrying the stories tied for first in a kind of horserace. A third station that had paid no attention to what it considered the nonstory finished a distant third.

Lest it appear that viewers were attracted to a "nothing" story, note that the information, although lacking facts, was colorfully presented. There were:

- extensive interviews with a former FBI agent who announced that a nearby county was a "hotbed of satanic activity";
- predictions of mass graves of human sacrifices, speculatively tying them to the murders by executed serial killer Ted Bundy;
- graphics of pentagrams and inverted crosses, close-ups of animal mutilations, and heavy-metal music.

The story was covered, according to one news director, "from beginning to end by our most experienced reporter. . . . It is a continuing story. The fact that bodies haven't been found yet is completely irrelevant."[12]

Such stories are typical of what is often labeled "tabloid journalism," mixing the sensational with the more common local news. Are they justified? Consider that sensationalism makes news more attention-getting or attractive to easily bored viewers. What are the values on each side of the position of using or not using sensational stories?

Discussions with the news staff at the TV stations have revealed to me that the print media exploit criticism of the kinds of stories that appear during sweeps periods in a way that is quite out of line. The effect of sensational stories on ratings is quite likely greatly over-rated.

BUDGET CUTTING AND BROADCAST NEWS

Another economic factor shaping the direction of broadcast news is the fact that as more media compete, there are fewer advertising dollars for each medium to share. Revenues generally drop for radio and television stations alike. When that happens, the stations must cut their budgets, and they allocate fewer budget dollars to news operations—sometimes with dismaying results.

How are broadcast news ethics being guided by budget restrictions, which are unwelcome to all parties in the operation? The answer can be seen by looking at the alternatives to traditional reporting that many stations are using to cut costs.

Many smaller radio stations that once took community pride in their local news operation have had to cut reporting staffs, often down to nothing. Many newscasts have come to rely on the national networks, thereby avoiding local news events altogether. Some stations will simply relay reworded versions of what appeared in the local newspaper.

"Street reporters" are being trimmed even from larger stations, often leaving news staff to rely for news on public relations agents or hired publicists who write news stories with an eye toward promoting the specific organization that hired them. Such "news development" often lacks the rigor and objectivity that once was the pride of some stations.

Many stations are turning to new technologies or other innovative techniques that bypass staff members. For example, a single reporter-videographer who uses a camcorder can do the job that two or three (with a soundman) had done before. Some people would argue that spreading a reporter's time and energy over many more tasks dilutes his or her abilities as a journalist.

Some stations have added the tasks of former staff members onto those of remaining personnel. One news reporter's title was changed to "news supervisor"—and he thereafter was expected to work twelve-hour shifts. He was to take his scanner home with him afterward in order to keep abreast of ongoing police activities that he should pursue. He was paid some monetary bonuses, but the station still reaped great savings over what it had had to pay the former staffer in salary.

Maintenance engineers have been cut, necessitating that reporters jerry-rig their equipment to make sure it works well enough to be usable. This perhaps distracts them from their reporting chores.

Rather than go out on the street, some reporters remain at the TV station and use telephone reports. They go out only for visually dramatic stories.

One reporter may be assigned several beats; court reporting or more mundane but important events that are of less interest to the public may be avoided out of necessity.

Rather than invest in permanent, full-time employees, management may use short-term or part-time employees. Student interns, eager to break into the media, will often work for no monetary recompense or only for college credit. Although it is not supposed to happen according to most labor agreements, such personnel replace paid staff members and cut costs for bottom-line-conscious management.

Because of the overabundant job market, seasoned anchors seeking higher wages—and in a big market, that can amount to considerable sums of money—are simply replaced by less expensive talent from smaller markets, or by young men and women from the hordes of attractive, often talented newcomers eager for a break. The personnel turnover in broadcast news may be higher than in most professions for this reason, which has little to do with ability or talent but everything to do with budget and economics.

Thirty- or 60-minute newscasts contain more ads, more promotions, more weather, more anchor chat, and more furnished video news releases than previously. It all can reduce the expense of rigorous hard reporting and result in an attractive, fast-paced newscast that is much different from journalism as previously understood.

FROM PRESS RELEASE TO VNR

In 1990 the golden arches of McDonald's opened in Moscow, Russia. Over 20 million people saw and heard about it on the news. You may remember a particular story that showed long lines of Russians waiting, the Russian menu, the Russian servers. This story was created not by news reporters covering the Russian capital but by a public relations firm working in behalf of McDonald's, Patterson-Parkington First International of Toronto. The story had been created as if it were a news story rather than a public relations event. It was distributed via a satellite service, Medialink, which calls itself a "video news release advisory network."

Recently we have entered the era of the *video news release*, or VNR, mostly without knowing much about it or realizing how it is mixed with our regular fare of TV news. For years, editors looked askance at press releases handed out by public relations agents, whom editors considered "hacks" paid to promote a point of view rather than what they regarded as an objective presentation of the truth. In fact, press releases often went right into the round file—the wastebasket—rather than be used seriously as news stories. But as news staffs were trimmed, press releases came to be used more often. Press releases, after all, were a source of information.

Then came a vast improvement over the typed press release: the news release carefully produced on video and delivered right into the facilities of a TV station by satellite.

Case Study 7.6: The "Easy" Journalism of VNRs

Most news editors still view VNRs with suspicion. But misgivings are dwindling, and their use is becoming more common. After Iraq invaded Kuwait in 1990, the group Citizens for a Free Kuwait used some of Kuwait's vast wealth to hire the public relations firm Hill and Knowlton to produce visuals of the Iraqi invasion, and later, of human rights violations in Kuwait. Some of the footage was shot by journalists, but the VNR was effectively placed and its distribution skillfully orchestrated by a careful strategy, lots of effort, and even more money. Over 80 million viewers saw one or both of the stories crafted by Hill and Knowlton and distributed by Medialink. The effect, as we know, was the U.S. entry into the Gulf War.

What challenge to conventional ethics may such a flow of information present? Here are some issues to consider:

1. Is there anything wrong with stories crafted by public relations people rather than journalists?
2. Is there room for compromise—perhaps using the VNR's footage but using a more independent, objective version of the accompanying story? Or using the VNR, accompanied by titles identifying it as such?
3. Are VNRs a legitimate source of information, or do they have some kind of inherent taint? Do they adulterate good material and pollute the objective truth? Or is information still information, regardless of its source?
4. In our information society, we come to rely more and more on the briefer—the person who can digest and condense all this information for us so we do not have the overwhelming task of trying to assimilate it all ourselves. In the age of the briefer, why not use such briefers as are found in the VNRs?
5. VNRs allow news staffs to concentrate on other important stories of their choice and act as free additional staff support. Is that not a smart use of resources, in a time of budget cutting? Is there really anything wrong with that?

THE ISSUE OF PRIVACY IN BROADCAST NEWS

It is only during the last century that our densely populated nation has become conscious of privacy laws—ensuring people the right to be left alone. But what happens when a person is a subject of public fascination, like a movie star, a musical artist, a football coach, or a millionaire businessman? It could also be a public official—a governor, a presidential candidate, a U.S. senator—all people who have chosen to put themselves in the spotlight to seek public office.

Public fascination with celebrities is amplified by seeing and hearing these figures on television. TV has a way of revealing to us even those people's very lifestyles, shown sometimes in glowing detail. When public figures are not the subject of TV news reports, private figures, by some twist of fate, become the subjects of such stories.

There are plentiful examples in the media today.

The identity of the alleged rape victim of William Kennedy Smith was protected during TV coverage of the 1991 trial by the use of a "blue dot" over the victim's face. But her name was ultimately disclosed in a news report by NBC News and the *New York Times,* causing a mild row. The releasing media's reasoning was that her name was a matter of public record anyway. Nearly all those who watched the televised reports did not know who she was, but there was still a fascination in discovering her name.

Many Americans spent part of the summer of 1991 watching the Senate Judiciary Committee hearing on the confirmation of Supreme Court nominee Clarence Thomas and his accuser of sexual harassment, Anita Hill. Hill embodied the problem that many women dread—glaring publicity for anyone bold enough to go public with accusations of harassment. Certainly Hill's anonymity, if not her reputation, was lost. Her privacy was penetrated by the media, even if at her own choosing.

Presidential hopeful Gary Hart, in 1988, challenged reporters to follow him if they had any questions about his character. They took him up on the dare, with disastrous results for Hart, who was spotted aboard his yacht with model Donna Rice. And the public knew it was more than press hype, for TV pictures showed the setting.

In the spring of 1992, television news went wild showing pictures of Gennifer Flowers, the woman who claimed to have had a long-running affair with Bill Clinton. Press conferences included a confession and a series of stories too compelling for the press to avoid. Clinton denied all of it, and as the presidential campaign went on, the claim receded into dim memory.

Basketball superstar Magic Johnson and tennis great Arthur Ashe both had to answer to the media not only for the fact that they had tested HIV positive for AIDS but for how they contracted it. Johnson had to admit to intimate details about his sexual and social life. Ashe explained that he had contracted the disease through a blood transfusion, probably from his heart operations. In both cases, TV news viewers were treated to footage of each performer in action in his respective sport, as if to jog our memories about their sports prowess. In some instances, a bizarre juxtaposition of sports action was mixed with a discussion of AIDS.

There are dozens of other examples as well. For example, it is not unusual for pictures of dead bodies or wounded victims suddenly to be displayed across the nation on television, regardless of whether viewers want or expect it.

The question here is whether such prying by the news media, especially television, is a violation of ethics of some kind. If so, by what standard? Is the ethical premise to be "If you wouldn't want your privacy invaded in this way, you should not invade others' privacy"? Or: "If it's of interest to the person in the street or the typical viewer, go for it. The more sensational, the better, since it should attract more viewers."

Just what guides news values in broadcasting, anyway? How much, if any, consideration is given to ethics in news judgments?

Although these are key questions, there are no pat answers to them, no common response that news directors give. Judgment is often individual, and some TV stations carry stories that others won't touch. This situation is complicated by the fact that so many stories are channeled through central distribution networks. For example, only one camera photographed the beating of Rodney King in Los Angeles that night. But all the networks eventually showed it—all, of course, from the same tape. Such showings seemed to override the judgment of any news director who may have objected to the scene of violence on the tape. It quite possibly is true that the potential magnitude of the act of an African-American being beaten by white police loomed larger than concerns of violence. But who decided that? On what basis was it decided?

Case Study 7.7: TV Covers a Suicide

A few years ago, a local political figure in Pennsylvania named R. Budd Dwyer was charged with fraud. Dwyer held a press conference. It was supposed to be a quick and routine announcement, presumably about his resignation from office.

It was held in the late afternoon; some children who were usually watching cartoons on TV saw the press conference instead. Dwyer rambled a bit, prompting some reporters to begin taking down their equipment and get ready to leave. He warned them not to leave just yet. He stuck his hand into a large manila envelope and pulled out a handgun. Amid cries of alarm, he warned people to stay away. Dwyer brought the pistol in front of his face, put the barrel into his mouth, and pulled the trigger.

Quickly and unpredictably, a gory scene unfolded that was visible to stunned TV viewers, including children, who were watching the purported press conference live. It did not take long for the television to cut away.

Although coverage of the suicide was accidental, the video recording of the event was subsequently used. In an effort to gain a little notoriety by having a local event aired nationally, the TV stations offered the recording to network editors. Suicides occur every day, even occasionally by locally well-known figures. Did Dwyer's suicide have the news value of a *national* story? No, the news value here likely lay in the fact that TV cameras had *witnessed* such a tragedy.

If you are a news editor, do you show the suicide shooting on TV? If you do not, you have no story. If you do, how do you handle such a situation without greatly offending viewers? To some editors, the offer of this eyewitness recording seemed just too good to pass up. What would you do?

Here is what really happened. After some discussion, a group of editors decided that there must be some way to use technology to screen offensive images of the event yet convey the drama of the moment. Eventually the story made its way to network news. Here's how: Viewers heard the story explained; they saw Dwyer wave the gun and warn others to stay away. Then, in the unfolding of the event, state-of-the-art technology "froze" Dwyer's image the moment before he put the gun in his mouth. But the audio carried on. Viewers *heard* the cries, "Oh my God, don't do it!" Then they *heard* the shot, followed by cries and screams. The reporter *narrated* what had happened, and sounds of the event were heard, but viewers were not privy to *seeing* the visual of what happened.

Somewhere in the decision-making process of photojournalism or TV news reporting, the gatekeepers—the editors—understand that visual material carries much more power than a spoken or written narrative. Ethics codes usually reflect such an understanding.

In reality, there are two people who make decisions about visual material: the photographer or videographer who selects and frames, and the editor who selects materials for media broadcast. The photographer's mission is to shoot, to get as many shots or as much coverage as possible. There is little time to ask questions about propriety or whether the shooting invades someone's privacy. Shoot, and ask questions later! One might always decide *not* to use images, but that is a later decision. That judgment will be made by a photo editor or news director. Still photos can be cropped. Video footage can be precisely edited to blur out parts of images, or precise editing can cut a few seconds or even a split-second of a moving image.

Newer technology can manipulate, superimpose, and juxtapose images that were not originally part of reality. We may not mind so much if Humphrey Bogart or Louis Armstrong appears to be a living part of a Coca-Cola commercial through the magic of computerized images. But what ethics will come into play when such images are manipulated for news programs? Perhaps that will not be done, after all—or perhaps it has already been done without our knowledge.

So much of the news we get comes to us by television that many of us have come to use television to define the world around us. We ourselves may not have had firsthand experience with the Middle East or Eastern Europe, but we may feel we know about the situation there because of the news media. Especially for events that are visual or spectacular, we rely on television. The Gulf War of 1991 with its "smart bombs" and Patriot missiles seemed perfectly suited to television coverage.

Often if there's a news story of visual interest—a fire, a spectacular traffic accident, or an airline disaster—we may seek out television to bring us the sights as well as the information about the story, even if we can get more details from a print medium. Not only do the images seem to give us more information, but in a sense they come to be a *confirmation of reality.* TV news producers realize this and cater to this need by using specially designed computer software to create such graphics as animated images, able to replicate, for example, what may have happened when an airplane crashed.

Case Study 7.8: Constructing the World by Television

As news director of a local TV station, you work with the assignment editor to determine the stories for the day's newscast—the mix of stories, which ones should be positioned as the important top "lead" stories, and which events of that day will be omitted. As you figure out the day's schedule, you make value judgments and some small-scale ethical decisions. Your options include the following:

1. You may place stories of political importance in the lead, even though they are not very interesting visually. (This may result in lower ratings—viewers can turn to competing stations to find more visually exciting stories.)
2. You may place stories in the lead that are visually interesting but that do not have much true news value or are not of consequence to very many people: an accident on the freeway, a garage burning down, police making drug arrests in a faraway city, and the like. (This might result in pretty good ratings, but your role will be more that of a panderer than a journalist.)
3. You may prominently position business news, featuring advertising clients or potential clients: the grand opening of a new supermarket, or the expansion of a local business hiring twenty more workers. (This may well result in advertising that pays the bills for all news stories.)

So how do you order the stories? How do you build the newscast in a way that reflects social responsibility, yet makes the newscast economically successful? Do the values of being watchdog for the public outweigh those of being a shrewd business person? Can one enlighten the public and yet cater to the demands of news in a pop culture setting?

Like many other professional settings in the mass media, one must decide the ever-haunting question: To what extent do a person's values or ideals dictate his or her functioning? Does one remain faithful to an ideal, regardless of professional circumstances, or do the practical necessities of a situation dictate the values? These are questions that will return again and again to the media practitioner for reexamination.

While answering the question of how to prioritize values in media news settings seems endless, there are clearly a number of ethical dilemmas dealing with broadcast news:

-   Should there be control of the free, unrestricted flow of information in the media to ensure a fair, balanced competition in an economic sense?

- Does the broadcast journalist have a role of social responsibility? If so, how should the growing influence of advertising over TV news be regarded? Are the values set down by Murrow and Friendly still valid today?
- Does a journalist's obligation to balance a story destroy his or her freedom?
- What is the role of government in overseeing the responsible, even ethical conduct of journalists?
- Can broadcast journalists ethically avoid balance? Is there room for "advocacy journalism"?
- To what extent should a reporter's personal relationships with the subject of a story affect its outcome?
- Is the sensationalizing of stories unethical?
- To what extent should business demands shape news, especially in times of budget crises and expenditure cuts?
- Can legitimate journalism come from sources promoting vested business or public relations interests?
- When (if ever) should the media's need to get a good story take precedence over an individual's right to privacy?
- How can broadcasting reflect socially responsible journalism and yet be economically successful?
- Finally, to what extent can one remain faithful to an ideal, yet work in a practical professional setting that often challenges those ideals?

Other questions associated with radio and television journalism, such as the relationship of professional codes to professional conduct, are considered elsewhere in this book.

Note how many of the above questions have the quality of "oughtness"—that is, they ask what *should* be done. There is often no *right* answer that arrives at a distinct position of Truth. Rather, there are merely reflections of values of media practitioners. But realizing the array of values to be considered is an important early step in our critical analysis of ethical dilemmas.

NOTES

1. Edward R. Murrow, address to the Radio/Television News Directors Association Convention, Chicago, Illinois, Oct. 15, 1958; reprinted in

Harry J. Skornia, *Television and Society* (New York: McGraw-Hill, 1965): 230.
2. Ibid., 235.
3. Ibid., 237.
4. Fred W. Friendly, *Due to Circumstances Beyond Our Control* (New York: Random House, 1967): 257. This work contains a detailed account of the event and the surrounding circumstances.
5. The FCC has interpreted the Fairness Doctrine thus: "The licensee, in applying the fairness doctrine, is called upon to make reasonable judgements in good faith on the facts of each situation, as to what viewpoints have been or should be presented, as to the format and spokesmen to present the viewpoints, and all other facets of such programming." 40 FCC 598—"Fairness Primer."
6. Article I, Radio/Television News Directors Association, Code of Broadcast News Ethics.
7. Red Lion Broadcasting Co. *v.* FCC, 381 F2d 908 (1967); aff'd 395 U.S. 367 (1969).
8. In the foreword to Andrea Arnold, *Fear of Food: Environmentalists' Scams, Media Mendacity, and the Law of Disparagement* (Bellevue, Wa.: Free Enterprise Press, 1990).
9. Ibid., 1.
10. Ibid., 126.
11. Ibid.
12. As quoted in Mary Mapes, "Rating Problem? Let Satan Help," *Washington Journalism Review,* Jul./Aug., 1989, p. 10.

8

Advertising Practices and Ethics

Like many of the other practices in radio and television broadcasting, advertising reflects changing ethical standards. Consider the following:

- In the early days of radio, advertising was not allowed during the evening hours, when the *family* was doing "serious" listening.
- In the early days of television, most commercials were 60 seconds long; some were two minutes long. Today that is rare.
- Before 1970, radio and television advertised cigarettes heavily. That year, Congress prohibited cigarette advertising in broadcasting. It is still allowed, of course, in print media.
- In earlier days of broadcast advertising, no mention was made of competing products or services. Now, Pepsi commercials, for example, are likely to take a crack or two at Coke.
- In earlier days, all bra commercials on television were produced using mannequins. Today live models are used.
- In earlier days, personal products such as feminine hygiene products were not advertised on the air. Today that is common.
- In the early days of television, advertising was held to 6 minutes per hour during prime time. Today, that has increased to 10 minutes per hour.

Advertising has grown from a modest entrepreneurial activity to become the giant economic influence it is today, when advertising revenues are well over $100 *billion,* or roughly two percent of the U.S. gross national product. Former advertising executives look back on their practices and admit the only real *value* of the profession has been making money.[1]

One historian has noted, "The advertising industry actually established the standards we live by and die by in this country, and yet there is not one adman in one hundred who knows he's doing anything more than selling catsup or soap.... You who are so effective and skillful in the art of communications, are so inept in communicating any sense of values."[2]

There are other more positive attitudes about advertising, however. After all, no smart advertiser would really want to work against the grain of American values or culture. That just would not pay.

TELEVISION ADVERTISING STANDARDS

Television advertising standards are reflected in these statements from network standards and practices policies:

> It is the policy of Capital Cities/ABC, Inc. to present advertising which is truthful and tasteful and not misleading or deceptive. This policy is not only mandated by our obligation as broadcasters to operate in the public interest, convenience and necessity, and by state and federal laws and regulations, but as a matter of good corporate citizenship.

The "obligation" this Capital Cities/ABC policy mentions comes partly from legal guidelines, partly from professional expectations, and partly from the ethical integrity of the corporate management. Just such mixtures shape ethics policies in the corporate world of telecommunications and advertising.

The business orientation of network television—that is, advertising—nonetheless has more to do with ethics policies than many other considerations. As has been said before, if a media corporation cannot muster sound economics from its advertising policies, it simply will not survive, no matter how noble its intentions.

With this economic orientation and the idea that *ethics* generally focuses on individual values, there are inherent ethical conflicts in advertising. The case studies in this chapter are designed to show some such conflicts, even dilemmas.

Case Study 8.1: Influencing Media Content

"What would you have done?" one producer asked. "Here's my story.

"It was the early 1970s, and there had been congressional hearings on televised violence and its relationship to antisocial behavior. The network toned things down a bit, but that lasted only for a while. Then it flared up again. That was followed by concerned consumer groups acting to pull advertisers into the issue. One group counted episodes of televised violence, noted which programs were the most violent, and observed the advertisers on those programs. Then the group published a list of those who 'supported violence' by advertising placement. Makers of shampoos and coffee soon found threats of boycotts if they did not steer away from such violence-laden programs. Our program was one of those.

"The advertising agency even went so far as to issue warnings to potential network advertisers telling them that they might meet with consumer displeasure if they bought advertising in or adjacent to certain programs.

"When we advised our writers of the problem, they were furious: 'No one tells us what we can and can't write!' Yet the network executives made it very clear that the program would not be carried if it discouraged advertising support.

"What would you do? Our choices were either to insist on less violence, resulting in the loss of our ingenious creative staff of writers who had made the program successful and innovative. Or, we could keep their ideas (violent as they might be) and face a possible consumer boycott."

The producer may not have had strong feelings one way or the other about violence, except as a problem to be resolved or as something that got in the way of smooth operations. Others who feel strongly about the issue of violence or who, like the writers, resent having their work "censored," might have inserted their own value judgments and taken a stronger stand.

How do you order priorities here? Is freedom of expression more important than control of depictions of antisocial violence? Or is freedom of expression to be subordinated when critical issues of economic welfare are at stake, in this case the advertising "support" of violence?

There remain taboo areas in our culture, yet the forbidden somehow seems very tempting. Advertisers make use of this fact. Remember the TV commercials where Mr. Whipple told us "Please don't squeeze the Charmin"? The prohibition against squeezing produced just the opposite response in viewers—the desire to squeeze—in an ingenious strategy that induced consumers to check out the tactile qualities of the tissue. Why does being taboo bestow an appealing enticement on a product?

Case Study 8.2: Should Broadcasters Advertise Condoms?

Currently, there is special fascination with the problem of whether to advertise condoms in the mainstream media. By now, public opinion on offering condoms in school health clinics has shifted to the point that over half respond positively in polls (53 percent).[3]

A few years ago, surveys indicated that the public felt that it was all right for television stations to show commercials for condoms, although at the time only about one-third of all stations indicated a willingness to accept condom advertising. The younger the respondent in the sample, the more likely he or she was to answer positively to allow stations to air condom ads. (Seventy-six percent of respondents ages 18–34 were in favor, but only 43 percent of those aged 65 and over.[4])

In an industry survey of 1,250 adults conducted by Louis Harris Associates, 72 percent said they would not be offended by television advertising of contraceptives (not necessarily condoms). The survey, sponsored by Planned Parenthood, also reported that 74 percent of the adults questioned said they favored using TV ads to promote the use of condoms to prevent the spread of AIDS.[5]

In a poll conducted in June 1992, on the other hand, *TV Guide* found that there are four products that fall into disfavor when advertised on TV: condoms, beer and wine, feminine hygiene products, and 900 telephone numbers. Of these four, however, the least objectionable was condoms; only 34 percent felt that they should not be advertised on TV.[6]

Despite more lenient public opinion, most TV stations today do not advertise condoms, although about 35 percent do. They are not prohibited from doing so, but they do not do so as a matter of practice.

What are the reasons for broadcasters' reluctance to advertise condoms? Would condom advertising promote sexual promiscuity? Are the reasons for not advertising condoms personal, social, professional, or simply arbitrary? Are they valid?

Case Study 8.3: Sex Can Sell Anything?

Anne Klein is a line of women's clothing. When Anne Klein awarded the Wieden and Kennedy Advertising Agency its account, the agency devised a plan whereby the clothes being advertised were not actually shown. Innovative copy, dreamy photography, blues-style music, and a soft voice-over created a feeling that the creators thought women liked. One report of the campaign was given by *Media Inc.*: "One of the most engaging and controversial spots describes, in detail, each piece of clothing that 'Sally' wore during the day, while Sally sits in her underwear atop a man and undoes her bra."[7]

The report goes on to quote the copywriter for the spots as saying that showing the clothes seemed redundant; it seemed natural *not* to show what was being sold.

The result? Women went into retail stores asking for the clothes after they saw the spots on TV. But the success was not as widespread as had been hoped. The "Sally" spots proved to be a bit too provocative for prime-time television and ended up airing only after eleven P.M.

Consider: With such a successful ploy, why should the stations air the spots only after eleven o'clock? Are there values concerning promiscuity that would offend large segments of the audience? Exactly how does one find out what will offend viewers, especially when there seem to be indications of creativity and success in the sexy design of this commercial? What kinds of values, if any, ought to get in the way of success, anyhow?

SEX AND ADVERTISING

It is easy for people to think that sexual inducements run counter to their value systems. However, perhaps the real appeal of advertising is that it uses sexual inducements to stroke values of which the viewer is only dimly aware.

An observer of the human psyche and its institutions was Erich Fromm, a psychologist and social critic. He said that the driving force in human behavior, especially consumer behavior, is *fear*—the fear of not being loved. There is a universal need for love, and advertising assures us that if we use a product, we will be loved. Indeed, the theme of many commercials is that gaining love depends on a gadget. In those moments when commercials influence us, we do not think rationally, Fromm said, but irrationally. Advertising fosters the idea, Fromm claimed, that it is neither human power nor human effort that creates the good life, but *gadgets*. Products promise us eternal youth, which guarantees us the love and happiness we want, and televised images of the beautiful person, good-looking, strong, active and full of energy, create the illusion of youth that never ages.

"Advertising," Fromm said, "tends to make a person greedy, to create the man who wants more and more, instead of trying to be more and more. Thinking—rational thinking, critical thinking, independent thinking—is undermined.... advertising ... does not try to inform and convince, but to suggest in a semi-hypnotic way. ... Since there is very little love in our society, sex plays a tremendous role."[8]

If people's need for love and sex helps sell products, does this theme tend to make sexual activity or promiscuity as attractive as the products being advertised? In other words, is advertising responsible for the popularizing of sex in society?

Some may reply, "Why not? It's been blamed for everything else." The answers remain elusive.

ALCOHOL AND ADVERTISING

Another social problem that more people and groups are beginning to blame on advertising, particularly TV advertising, is the excessive consumption of beer and wine.

In a recent Gallup poll, 34 percent of respondents thought that beer advertising was targeted at minors, and 39 percent felt that beer advertising should be banned.[9] Those who have studied the social problems caused by alcohol abuse can find widespread evidence of its evils.

Reasons to End Beer and Wine Commercials

Alcohol problems kill the equivalent of a 747 airplane seating 300 people every day, 365 days of the year.[10] Problems of broken homes, child abuse, and crime often are linked to alcohol abuse, while conventional medical evidence linking alcohol with assorted health hazards is overwhelming and uncontroversial.

While it is difficult to accurately pinpoint the advertising expenditures of breweries, it is safe to say that the figure resides well into the *billions* of dollars.

If television sells beer and encourages beer drinking, should it be held responsible for helping to promote a source of many of our social ills? Just how can broadcasters keep their lucrative income from beer and wine advertising yet remain blameless in promoting a social activity that is often both self-destructive and socially destructive?

Health organizations, including the American Medical Association, have called for an outright ban on beer and wine advertising on television, especially during the telecasting of sports events that are seen by large numbers of teens. Groups that stop short of an outright ban insist that a health-hazard warning label should be put on both labels and advertising. Beer advertising thus would be put into the same category as commercials for tobacco products.

Such groups assume that beer advertising has a strong persuasive influence on young consumers. The models in TV commercials appear to be young, fun-loving, attractive, and engaged in activities desirable to many young people. Although it is illegal in most states for anyone under 21 years old to purchase and consume alcohol, advertising is often pitched in college media, where about 65 percent of the market is under 21. In most realms of media marketing, that would be a poor strategy unless a significant chunk of that 65 percent was a target market. In fact, according to the National Clearinghouse of Alcohol and Drug Information, U.S.

college students spend some $4.2 billion a year on alcoholic beverages.

Moreover, critics point out, alcohol advertising contains mostly imagery associated with happy times and little valuable consumer information. The purchase of a six-pack offers the hope of good times and social acceptance—an escapist promise that often leads to addiction and sometimes to alcoholism.

Reasons to Keep Beer and Wine Ads on the Air

The ills of beer and wine advertising seem clear and definitive to its critics. But there are some serious principles to consider from another perspective.

First and most fundamental is the issue of the First Amendment. Advertising ("commercial speech," in legal jargon) is protected by the First Amendment; it is a form of free expression. The government has no right to censor speech, despite its possible negative social consequences. If a product causes harm or is inherently evil, consumers will reason that out and shun the product, according to democratic and libertarian ideals. The decision to screen something out should be made on the consumer or citizen's end, not on that of the government.

Second, if beer and wine advertising is banned, what is to prevent the censor's ax from falling on other products as well whose consumption presents health risks of one kind or another—sugared cereal, meat or milk with fat content, or even automobiles, in which tens of thousands of Americans die every year?

Third, the anti-advertising arguments assume that there is a causal relationship between advertising and use of the product, including abuse. If advertising did not affect consumer purchasing behavior, those favoring a ban argue, breweries would not spend millions of dollars each year in such ventures. To this, advertisers and marketers will reply that such advertising does not necessarily induce consumption, but only encourages those already consuming beer to use the brand that is being advertised.

Finally, there are financial arguments. Breweries and wineries have an enormous economic stake in the continuation of advertising. Of course, so do the media and the associated industries—advertising agencies, creative and production people, and so on.

Case Study 8.4: Is There Some Compromise?

Suppose you are in a position to decide whether a TV station will run beer and wine commercials. Is there a "golden mean" that you can reach that somehow gives satisfaction to both sides of the beer and wine argument? Except for those who dogmatically argue either extreme, you might find a solution somewhere in the middle. You might run the commercials but use the industry practice of "disclosure advertising," or a warning not to drink and drive, cautions against overconsumption and possible alcoholism, and the like. As a matter of fact, disclosure advertising may actually be more beneficial to the side advocating an advertising ban, since it would publicize the very misgivings that initiated the ban in the first place.

If your station's alcohol advertisers feel that disclosure advertising would adversely affect sales or destroy the popularity of their product, you could then demonstrate your responsibility by airing public service announcements with warnings of abusive drinking.

Since this issue has recently been of great concern to broadcasters, case studies of specific strategies in dealing proactively with it are discussed in Chapter 10.

ADVERTISING ON CABLE TELEVISION

We often assume that advertising restrictions for television are universal, that even cable TV advertising must not go beyond the borders set for broadcast TV. The way we think about this has perhaps been set by some historical factors.

- The earlier medium of broadcast television has been regulated by the FCC.
- TV networks and stations once had stringent policy guidelines set by NAB (see Chapter 4).
- Policies governing advertising agencies, which serve broadcast and cable TV clients alike, were formulated mostly before cable TV advertising became much of a force; creative strategies were designed for broadcast TV.

But the fact is that advertising restrictions for broadcast television may not apply to cable TV.

Case Study 8.5: Should Advertising Be Bolder on Cable TV?

In a sense, cable TV advertising is starting all over again in a relatively new world. And this time, it could be starting with a new perspective of social mores, free of what some may consider "hangups" of an earlier generation.

Since cable TV is not governed by any restrictions associated with broadcast TV, products that are not advertised on broadcast TV might well be considered on cable TV: hard liquor, gambling casinos, perhaps even tobacco products. More daring advertising approaches and creative strategies might be used—for example, nudity or questionable language.

Such new products and techniques might get enough attention that cable TV could make its own inroads as a unique advertising medium. And since cable is now becoming a viable advertising medium, it might greatly enhance the market share of some products. With the promise of greater revenues and more attention on Madison Avenue, why would cable not want to exploit its freedom?

What are the ethics involved?

Do the values of an earlier generation apply? The same individual values and social mores that set things up fifty years ago are generally still strongly in place. Concerns about products and techniques that are taboo for broadcast TV advertising remain.

Or should new, bolder advertising standards be established for cable TV, in which cable, without qualm, advertises hard liquor and uses nudity? Whether such taboos ought to be abandoned is arguable. Consider the arguments on each side of the question. One is likely to become quite enlightened about his or her value system from such a discussion.

ADVERTISING AND ETHICS

Radio and TV advertising can be economically and socially productive and enriching. But it can also exhibit negative facets, including everything from irritation to widespread deceit and exploitation. Our economy cannot live without it; neither can the media.

What, then, is to be made of the criticisms of radio and TV advertising: its excesses, its influence on the content of the media, the creation of false needs, the exploitation, the stereotyping, the appeals to the irrational? Are these issues to be ignored? Or are they to be magnified?

Here lie the fundamental questions intricately involved in the relationship between advertising and ethics.

Often our values are so tightly interwoven with the products we consume that it becomes difficult to segment and analyze them. We value the human spirit, but a Spirit is also an automobile. Love may be the greatest Christian virtue of all, but it is also a cosmetic, and, spelled a different way, it is a baby's diaper. And what is Life all about? It is a cereal, of course. Just what things do have merit? Merit—isn't that a cigarette?

Some Eastern Europeans may have found new freedom. But women at the supermarket have also found New Freedom—a sanitary napkin. And what of the quest for Truth? Well, True is a cigarette—low-tar, of course. And what is the ultimate satisfaction of life? One brewer assures us that where its beer is concerned, "It just doesn't get any better than this."

In describing the "idols of the marketplace," Father John F. Kavanaugh has described advertised products as a part of modern-day idolatry:

> The theological virtues have become commodified. Buicks are "something to believe in." "Hope (cosmetics) is all you need." "Trust Woolite." Love is a diaper, a bottle of Amaretto, a carpet shampoo.
>
> Thus the media-culture-economy formation is complete. We have not only a philosophy of human identity and human relationship collapsed into the world of buying and selling, we have a full blown theological system. The result is cultural ideology as idolatry.[11]

Those who concede that advertising is a form of idolatry may not mind such a connection. But even if you are concerned about the possibility of materialism in advertising, what do you do about it?

This brings us back to the previous question: What do we do with the criticism of advertising?

Perhaps in a free society, the best that can be done is to *educate* consumers and allow them to judge with their own value systems whether advertising is a spiritually threatening idolatry, a nuisance, or a vital economic stimulus.

In the end, linking values and ethics with our most common experience in the media—advertising—may turn out to be a vital but never-ending education.

Case Study 8.6: What Is Ethical Behavior in Advertising?—Some Collective Judgments from an Ethics Survey

When the Advertising Club of New York surveyed its members as to whether twelve specific advertising scenarios were ethical, *Advertising Age* magazine compared the results with the responses of its own readers. Below is one of the twelve cases posed to the professionals. Note your response, then look at their answers.

> Your agency is one of four semifinalists that have been asked to compete for a new product assignment from a major toy marketer. While your agency has experience in marketing to children, this assignment would be its first in the toy category, let alone for a leading manufacturer. During a final briefing your prospective client discloses that the "new product" is a set of war toys, complete with pseudo-ammunition, guns, and so on. Your agency decides that it will accept the assignment if it receives the award.

Is this ethical or not? Most advertisers had no qualms about seeing this as perfectly ethical:

	Ethical	*Unethical*
Agency	75%	25%
Advertiser	86%	14%
Media	73%	27%
Other	88%	12%

Note that those in the media were less likely than their advertising colleagues to find the situation ethical. Some respondents indicated that while it did not seem unethical, they personally would not do it. The results also noted that westerners saw it differently from southerners: 63 percent of the western-region respondents approved the war toy pitch, compared with 94 percent of those from the South.[12]

The response to this sample question reveals that even professionals with common goals have mixed attitudes, value systems, and perceptions about ethics. No questions in the survey revealed any kind of uniform view of conventional ethical standards. This may be a reflection of our pluralistic society. The results concluded that while there are some differences in geographic areas, no one region is uniquely unethical or strikingly different in its ethics from another. Also, no particular segment of the advertising business was significantly different from the ethical norm.

SUMMARY

This chapter has offered a glimpse into one of the places where the world of business converges with the mass media: advertising. Historically, it appears that the standards of ethics have changed. But whether those changes mean better or worse ethics often turns out to be a matter of individual interpretation. In some cases, there are professional expectations in the realm of ethics. But certainly there is no uniform perception, only issues.

Some of the issues identified in this chapter are the following:

1. The most basic clash—the economic engine and profit motive of the media versus the content that conflicts with it. Small-scale occurrences of this conflict happen all the time in the media, everywhere from small stations to metro-market settings. There undoubtedly always will be such conflicts. There is no overall guiding strategy that will work to resolve all situations. Each conflict has to be resolved with an eye to all the variables in the situation, including the value systems of the individuals involved.

2. Society has long had taboos. Certain behavior may be unacceptable, and that may relate to certain products (like condoms), to advertising a product (like hard liquor on television), or to the way a product is advertised (brassieres on live models).

3. Our inherent drives and basic instincts that include the sex impulses have been associated with products in advertising. Sex sells, even for a product that may have little to do with sex. Is such association as such unethical even when we have generally become quite accustomed to accepting such associations? Does that make it more ethical? Is there anything wrong with offering a product that appeals to an individual's great need to be loved?

4. If there are social problems brought about by alcohol abuse, even though alcohol is legal for purchase under most conditions, should there be curtailment of advertising it? When broadcast media have an important source of income in beer and wine advertising, how does a station manager respond to the idea of dropping it with an eye to public perception of his or her ethics? (Further strategies are discussed with respect to this issue in Chapter 10.)

5. Competent advertisers have always recognized differences among the various media in the selling of products. If those differences are associated with ethics practices, should advertisers seek

out media with different value positions? If cable TV is less concerned with traditional standards of advertising or products advertised, should the advertising be switched to cable? And if so, what is to be the response of broadcast TV?

6. As in any good business practice, a basic question continues to surface in broadcast media—what constitutes ethical behavior? To what extent are an individual's ethics a response to his or her colleagues' professional expectations, religious upbringing, and unwavering loyalty to specific values?

As advertising practices become more diverse, creativity more ingenious, and the media more dynamic, questions concerning ethics will multiply. Being prepared for these questions and their basic premises should help the media manager anticipate and make intelligent, rational, and defensible decisions in the future.

NOTES

1. See, for example, Jerry Della Femina, *From Those Wonderful Folks Who Gave You Pearl Harbor: Frontline Dispatches from the Advertising War* (New York: Simon and Schuster, 1970). Also Terry Galanoy, *Down the Tube* (New York: Pinnacle Books, 1972).
2. Keith Berwick, personal communication.
3. "Family Values," *Time* (Aug. 31, 1992): 26.
4. "Acceptability of Broadcasting Condom Advertising," a Research and Planning Memo of the National Association of Broadcasters (Jul.–Aug. 1987).
5. "74% Say Condoms Ads OK," *USA Today*, March 19, 1987.
6. "Would You Give Up TV for a Million Bucks?" *TV Guide* (Oct. 10, 1992): 17.
7. "W&K's Sexy Anne Klein Ads Heat up Sales," *Media Inc.* (Aug. 1991): 3A.
8. Erich Fromm, in "You and the Commercial," transcript of broadcast on *CBS Reports* (Apr. 26, 1973): 15, 16.
9. "Survey Shows 39% Favor Beer Ad Ban," *Advertising Age* (June 5, 1989): 6.
10. Statement of George Hacker, director for alcohol policies, Stop Marketing Alcohol on Radio and Television, in a panel entitled "Free Speech and Advertising—Who Draws the Line?" Institute for Democratic Communication, Boston University, April 1987; transcript.
11. John Kavanaugh, S.J., "Idols of the Marketplace," *Media and Values* 37 (Fall 1986): 5.
12. "Industry Ethics Are Alive," *Advertising Age* (Apr. 18, 1988): 88.

9

Ethics and Business Management in Telecommunications

In small cities throughout middle America, business has shifted from small, locally owned enterprises to large chain stores. Main Street has been vacated, while malls have arisen. Buildings housing modest businesses have been torn down, and banks have replaced them. The banks, too, have constantly changed their signs as they merge from local and regional banks to larger chains with increasing acquisitions. There are fewer self-employed workers and more payroll-dependent workers, who are prone to being laid off as the economy fluctuates.

So has it been with the media. Small radio stations, often owned by families or local entrepreneurs, are not making good profits. About half of all radio stations, most of them small, are *not* making profits, while others make only marginal profits. So for a reasonable price, they are sold to a company with far-reaching holdings. Television stations, once prohibited from being part of any organization that also had cable TV holdings or had more than a handful of other stations, are no longer subject to such restrictions. They are free to become part of a higher economic order where operational decisions are made not by the "people in the trenches of day-to-day battle" but by people in posh corporate offices.

This chapter offers a closer examination of the question of whether the media industry's fundamental efforts to earn a profit or stockholder dividends interfere with the media's mission of informing and serving the public.

At once, many observers would answer, "Not usually."

What, then, causes the question to arise in the first place? Here's a list of questions for discussion:

1. Does the vast wealth of some media holdings and their growing concentration in media conglomerates pose a threat to the autonomy of the messages relayed by those media? Just how much responsibility does a food corporation or a media mogul feel toward the social obligations of the media to enlighten or inspire?

2. *National* media seem to be the most economically viable. What happens to the traditional concept of "localism," or serving the city or market where a national medium is located?

3. Some of the reasons for government regulation of broadcasting are beginning to disappear with newer technologies such as cable TV. That has caused an era, over the last decade, of deregulation. Has deregulation now gone to such an extreme that regulation ought be to reinstituted, even at the possible expense of encumbering the *business* of telecommunication?

4. How long can a free country with ideals of justice survive when vast wealth is juxtaposed against pockets of poverty, unemployment, homelessness, and global famine? In such a situation can the media, with their vested economic interest in the status quo or in making greater profits, make inroads in addressing social problems?

5. Can "business reporting" really give a true picture of the economic scene when the businesses that are being reported on control the economic fate of the reporters?

THE DEBATE OVER MEDIA CAPITALISM

Here are some issues that arise in reply to these questions.

Arguments for Media Capitalism

1. The enterprising opportunities and the profit incentives of today's U.S. media make possible the growth and profit that form the capital that builds efficient, powerful media structures.

2. The U.S. media have long been the envy of media systems all over the world. Some socialist systems have moved to the sounder, better-financed systems of enterprise capitalism, modeling themselves after the U.S. system.

3. The capital provided by this system allows for new ideas and for corporate research and development. It fosters testing what's better and allows the public to decide which direction improvements and new technology will take.

4. An economically sound system, such as that in the United States, allows a healthy, multichannel flow of information, offering a rigorous marketplace of ideas, which basically strengthens democracy.

5. Such a healthy system also allows for a multichannel, diverse assortment of entertainment. A seemingly never-ending variety of cultural forms for any specialized interest can be addressed by this system, with its vast wealth of ideas and tastes.

6. Because the media have become such an important facet of the U.S. economy—selling goods and services, offering information, entertaining and educating—they play an important part in economic stimulation, keeping businesses (such as those associated with the media) healthy and the economy growing.

Arguments Against Media Capitalism

1. The media are no longer truly laissez-faire, free-enterprise, entrepreneurial structures. The small or modest-size media ventures are being swallowed up by larger corporations—big business. The media generally are in the hands of the wealthy.

2. The promise of starting a new mass media enterprise remains only a promise without vast wealth to support the effort. There really is no new enterprise anymore, except as extensions of already-existing empires.

3. The rapid concentration of media ownership poses a threat to both autonomy and diversity. Writing of *The Media Monopoly*, Ben Bagdikian warned in 1987, "If mergers and acquisitions by large corporations continue at the present rate, one massive firm will be in virtual control of all major media by the 1990s. . . . If all major media in the United States . . . were controlled by one 'czar,' the American public would have reason to fear for its democracy."[1]

4. The media, once highly competitive with one another—an element that drives the system—are losing that competitive edge because even competitors are becoming members of the same corporate family. TV stations in New York and San Francisco, for instance, that were once owned by Warner Communications, are now owned by Time-Warner, which controls magazines, films, publishing houses, cable systems, pay cable, production studios for motion picture and television, record companies, and comic books. Media that, at first glance, seem to be much different from each other might lose their diversity when they become members of the same group.

5. The general public knows only of positive attitudes toward the media's economic orientation. They lack information about media economic structures because the media are limited to telling only what their economic suppliers allow. We are kept ignorant by the economic blinds imposed by that system.

6. Business heads have become shy of bold or innovative projects and ideas that do not make substantial profits at first. Cuts in media operations are made solely on the basis of profits.

7. When profits must be maximized and "excess fat" trimmed, it is often investigative reporters or forward-looking research and development team members or untried ideas that are sacrificed. Such a process may be less the fault of "evil" CEOs than of the system that traps everyone—including the CEOs—into the mentality of more profit for the stockholders and a general striving on everyone's part for more money.

There are further arguments on both sides of the issue, but these seem to be the compelling "teasers" in media economics that many observers see as critical in the study and future direction of the media.

Case Study 9.1: Preparing for the Debate in Media Economics

As a television producer and researcher, you are preparing materials for an upcoming televised debate between a professor of media economics and the CEO of a media corporation. Your task is to dig out information and make suggestions to the participants to help make the event compelling and interesting.

First, you gather the evidence for each side, then highlight those issues that will evoke heartfelt feelings and strong rhetoric.

You must also be prepared to prompt the debate participants to respond to the challenges in these discussion questions:

1. What are the values or ethics on each side of the debate over media capitalism? Is it merely a matter of material hedonism—the material well-being and pleasure that come from economic security—versus a political and social benevolence that serves the political and social system?
2. Who is profiting from such strategies as employee and operational cuts: The manager who receives a salary bonus for maximizing profits? The stockholder who invests in media stock simply to increase the investment? The CEO who brings notoriety to the company for its no-nonsense, cost-cutting operation?
3. Are there value choices to be made here? Are the ethical problems those of the basic system, or do they involve only specific problems within the system? How can the media go beyond their economic orientation?

To these last questions, television producer Norman Lear replies:

> If American business insists upon defining itself solely in terms of its market share, profitability and stock price—if its short-term material goals are allowed to prevail over all else—then business tends to subvert certain moral-cultural values that undergird the entire system. Such values are social conscience, commitment to one's community, loyalty to one's company—in short, a sense of the commonweal. From the decline of public morality and personal values to the culture of narcissism to young people's inability to read and write, each of a hundred social ills originates with this trickle-down value system and its prevailing bottom-line mentality.[2]

Using Lear's statement, consider or discuss the macroissues of media economics. Using the material in this chapter, develop the arguments for and against media capitalism. Which side in this debate seems to have the most compelling arguments, and why? How would you construct these arguments?

ANTITRAFFICKING LEGISLATION

At one time, owning a broadcast station was a long-term commitment. To ensure that such a commitment was made, the FCC set *antitrafficking* policies, prohibiting the turnaround sale of a station in less than three years after first acquiring the license. The idea was that station licensees should hold a station for the purpose of serving its listening or viewing public, rather than to turn a profit by a quick resale.

In December of 1982 that antitrafficking rule was eliminated, transforming broadcast properties into investments. Station licensees now gained the flexibility to take advantage of buying and selling opportunities. The repeal led to a dramatic increase of "short-term trading" of broadcasting stations. In 1982, before the rule was dropped, fewer than 600 radio stations had been traded, with dollar volume of less than $500 million. By 1985, that had increased to 1,558 stations changing hands, for over $1.4 billion. In television, the same shift occurred. Thirty stations had been sold in 1982 for $527 million. The increase by 1985 had moved to 99 stations being sold for $3.29 billion. Group transactions went from zero in 1982 to 218 transactions in 1985, worth just under $1 billion.[3]

Stations, now dubbed "broadcast properties," were being sold and traded like pork bellies. While many such financial transactions were made by keen financial analysts who saw a great future in the development of broadcasting, others were made purely for profit, with little regard for the future of the "properties."

Those people with large financial holdings in broadcasting stations seemed happy with the change. Dropping the antitrafficking rule gave a great deal more flexibility to their financial holdings, trading, and liquidity.

Case Study 9.2: Deregulation Run Amok?

You are a small-market broadcaster, with three stations in your market of 80,000 people. Watching your competitors, you learn that one of the stations is selling to a group owner that is known for its cost-cutting, hyping of ratings, and quick turnaround sale of station properties. Sure enough, you soon find that one of the town's competing stations, with the backing of corporate funds, is pouring money into promoting the station and hyping the ratings.

Naturally, you are on the losing end. Your ratings are hurt. Everyone, it seems, is listening to this "new" station. Your advertising is worth less, and your station starts to lose money. There is not enough profit margin for you to invest heavily in the promotion of your own station. There seems to be little you can do, since this is all part of how free enterprise and capitalism work. It does not seem fair, but you stay in there fighting.

Then, a year after the original sale, the group owner resells. The value of the station has been hyped through its highly visible promotion, bringing higher ratings, higher advertising rates, and increased profits. Moreover, you discover that incredibly enough, the seller is asking twice its original purchase price. During its short tenure as owner the selling company has manipulated the monetary value of the station in such a way that it is now eager to sell for a handsome profit.

The FCC rules allowing "trafficking" of stations for relatively quick turnaround sale seems to give advantage to the group or corporate buyer—much to the disadvantage of the small business entrepreneur who stays loyal in the community but must compete with such economic unfairness.

"Does the playing field seem level here?" you think. Why would the FCC drop rules in order to favor the companies that have deep pockets, at the expense of the true entrepreneurs of our country, the small business? Is this what Reaganomics was all about? The change was all part of the Reagan administration's attempt to get government out of business, you're told. The result, although perhaps unfortunate to you, is part of how our capitalistic economy is supposed to work—no government intervention or policies to protect anyone, big or small.

You do not like it, but that's the system. Or is it? Can the system respond to its citizens who are hurt? Could the FCC be pushed to reinstate the antitrafficking rule? Or if that does not work, what about rallying support for legislation in Congress for statutory protection— laws codifying antitrafficking, which the FCC would be obliged to enforce? It would not be just FCC rules, as previously. This would seem to fit, from what you know about law. It's like the antitrust laws designed to prevent large businesses from overwhelming the survival of small businesses.

Where do your values place you on the scale of laissez-faire (no government intervention) versus regulation for the sake of fair competition?

Closely related to the antitrafficking issue is the issue of the opportunity of liquidity for long-time community broadcasters.

Case Study 9.3: Investment Return

What are the financial opportunities for broadcasters in the setting of small business? Put yourself into a scenario not uncommon in the mid-1980s or even today.

You own a radio station in a small market of about 100,000 people. You had acquired the station from your father, who was a broadcast pioneer in this part of the country in the early 1930s. Recently, you have invested in new equipment, giving better quality to your signal. It was an expensive investment, and it put the station into some heavy debt, but the venture seems to be paying off. There is good advertising support from the community, many of whom you know from the city's Chamber of Commerce and other associations in which you have invested time and energy.

Often, however, it seems that you are just not getting anywhere in the rat race. As soon as you pay this investment off, there will be other new technology that will require the same expenditure. It will not be many more years before you'll be looking toward retirement. Maybe you should get out now while there is still time to enjoy life, buy a bigger boat, and spend some time with your family.

One of your colleagues, a broadcaster in another part of the state, tells you of a reliable broker who would handle the sale of the station, paying a substantial sum that you could use for investments from which you could live without working—that is, being independently wealthy.

Deciding whether to sell is not easy, and it is not free from some deep, complicated issues that loom close to the heart. The station is part of your family legacy. It's not going to be easy to leave. Moreover, you're sure to miss the clients, the association, and the influence your radio station seems to have in the community.

You know from the way that new buyers often reorganize stations that there will likely be changes in your old staff. Faithful employees who have given years of devoted service to a profession they love will probably be shown the door. The job market is not secure right now; likely, it would be hard for many of them to find other work.

But why should you worry? The sale would bring you a lot of money—like winning the lottery! You'd be financially secure. You've worked hard all your life, and you deserve the pay-off from your hard work and investment in the station.

Perhaps there is a middle ground. Is it possible that one condition of the sale would be to keep existing employees or to guarantee other conditions about which you are concerned?

Such compromises would be unusual in such a sale. It is unlikely that a buyer would agree to such conditions, especially if that buyer is interested in profit-taking—cutting expenses, such as by hiring cheaper personnel.

What would you do? There is no easy way out of this dilemma, which literally hundreds of small broadcasters faced over the last decade or so. The decision you make may stem from your own value system. What are the values on each side of the decision of whether or not to sell?

SALES ETHICS

The fundamental building block of any business organization is its sales staff. If the sales staff and sales policies are not conscious of good ethical practices, the organization itself is built on a faulty base.

How does a salesperson know when a practice, seemingly beneficial for the organization, is not ethical? What kind of policies does management construct to address ethical practices?

Some business ethicists have suggested a checklist for determining ethical accountability for various practices.[4]

1. *Is the practice legal?* Most observers would agree that if it's illegal, it certainly is not ethical and should not be practiced, no matter what the short-term advantages might be.
2. *Is the practice fair?* Does it treat everyone equally? Are decisions made rationally, rather than emotionally, or based on associations other than business relationships?
3. *What does your conscience say?* Would there be any problem if your practices were widely publicized? An administrative policy should conform to the highest ideal of a noble character and enhance self-esteem and self-confidence.

Case Study 9.4: Telecommunications Sales Ethics

As sales manager of a TV station, you are aware that many stations use various rating scales to charge their advertisers for air time they buy. Generally, the more time an advertiser purchases, the cheaper it is per unit. Other practices favoring longtime, good customers include giving them better time availabilities, better production rates, and other good packaged deals. Because the deals vary widely, many stations choose to no longer publish rate cards or make rates publicly available.

You decide, however, that a more honest policy would be to publish and practice across-the-board pricing for all clients, regardless of their status. There would still be advantages for big buyers, but that would be published and known up front to everyone. The policy will be, "No special deals for friends or special clients." This policy seems more ethical to you, and you think it should appeal to the honest business person.

But your sales staff protests: "This policy cuts into our commissions—we're earning less! And it cuts into the station's profits as well! Go back to conventional practices—no one is going to notice this new 'policy of integrity' anyway. Are we not in business to make money for the station as well as for ourselves? Why should you construct policies to interfere with this?"

Is it unethical to deal in a less-than-straightforward manner? Is there anything wrong with giving special favors to good clients?

Perhaps no station manager has ever defined ethics in this manner. Is it up to you to do so? Are you blazing the trail for ethical practice in broadcast sales? What kind of philosophy guides your ideal that openness is akin to integrity, anyway? Consider the arguments of both sides of the issue, and determine what policy you would implement. Also consider: Can you administer business integrity by the policies you shape in your organization?

In his book on *Broadcast and Cable Selling,* Charles Warner notes:

A mission statement is a primary source of pride, self-esteem, and self-confidence for employees—they have confidence in knowing that their company knows where it is going and why it is going there. Mission statements that concentrate only on profits are counterproductive, as few employees give a hoot about how much richer owners become. Managing only for profits (or for making a budget) is like a hitter in baseball keeping his eyes on the scoreboard instead of on the ball.

If companies are run by accountants, bankers, lawyers, or investors with bottom-line, short-term values, then they are probably better off without mission statements and other communications that reveal their executive's values. Often these strictly bottom-line people are primarily interested in cash flow and assets, not in people. It is very difficult to convince bean counters that employees are a station/system's most important and valuable asset and that employees value other things, like community service and self-esteem, more than profits for the owners (in which the employees usually do not share).

If a company does not have a mission statement that gives it purpose, pride, values and direction, then salespeople should consider writing one for their own use. Once a meaningful mission statement is written, a code of ethics becomes easy to write and to follow—salespeople know what they are doing, where they are going, and, more important, why they are doing it. Purpose gives meaning to work.[5]

ETHICS AND JOB SECURITY

There is much to be said for the comfort of good wages: a home, security, the promise of a family, leisure activities like enjoying the arts, a college education for the children, a pension for retirement, plus many of the good conveniences of life. But pressed too far, seeking material wealth can become a kind of folly, of which generations of people have been warned. Greed, self-indulgence, luxury, pleasure, and a hedonistic lifestyle bring vapidity to life and shallowness to character. If business can claim that "we are best served by a system that runs lean and hungry," is that not true of our own lifestyle as well?

Case Study 9.5: Cost-Cutting and a Reporter's Future

Peter spent fifteen years of his life working first at small, then medium-size, then large-market TV stations. With help from some friends who admired his work and with some strokes of good luck, he got his break and was hired by a network as a correspondent. He made his name for two productive years. Then hard times hit the network, which was already being affected by cable. The predictable result was that the network made some deep cuts.

Rather than use its own cadre of correspondents, the network established alliances not only with its affiliates but with other stringers—part-time and amateur reporters who would contribute stories for considerably less recompense than full-time network correspondents.

The network closed many of its domestic bureaus but merged its facilities with its affiliates of owned stations. On foreign soil, it worked out alliances with the news services of other countries. The network arranged for satellite transmissions in harmony with the needs of its stations and included no more than absolutely necessary.

In all of this the network laid off nearly 300 workers, including news correspondents. Peter was one of them. Although he had had good experience, it was going to be hard for him to find a new, comparable position: The job market was flooded with other reporters who had been laid off and with recent graduates who seemed fired with enthusiasm.

Peter could always go back to a smaller station and practice his journalism there. Or he could simply give up on the whole idea of reporting. There were promises of working in the same network's sales department for as much money as he had earned as a journalist. But he was not especially fond of sales; he thought he was not the type.

Peter had to ask himself: Was he working for the love of news, or a job that would put bread on the table? If he stayed in journalism, how much security would there be? How long could he remain a "marketable product" in this often-transient industry? Some of his older colleagues had stayed with it long enough to retire early with good benefits—some even with the "golden parachutes." Peter was not old enough to retire yet. Should he stay with the network in another capacity until he was? Or should his work be the love of his heart—reporting?

Peter's heart was in broadcasting—in those parts that included writing, investigating, interviewing, and doing a good story not spotted by other reporters.

Peter considered the alternatives. The future of broadcasting was in the business end, it seemed to him, in sales, not in reporting. Was that a permanent shift in where the money was? He had seen the figures; inevitably, business and sales personnel were paid more than news people. But how dominant should the money aspect be in making his decision?

Just how strongly did Peter hold his values? How determined was he to go with his professional love and spurn a well-paying job where he could not place his whole heart? It seemed to be a matter of a personal preference based on his value system. What would your preference be? Why? How would you advise Peter?

BUYING POLITICAL INFLUENCE

For about a century now, whenever big business has become so big that it poses a threat to consumers, citizens, or the government, Congress has passed laws that mitigate its looming influence. When the oil companies threatened to become as large as the government itself, Congress passed antitrust laws. When Wall Street brokers conspired to work hidden avenues to make unfair profit, laws were passed to prohibit such activities. Even in a truly free-enterprise economy, the establishment and competition of business is "officiated" by a government that attempts to enforce fairness.

As the broadcasting industry evolved, the U.S. government set up the Federal Communications Commission to ensure that there were no unfair advantages in ownership, business practices, or even programming. In many ways the direction of the business of broadcasting was determined by the laws that kept it in check. Not unlike other businesses, broadcasting sought to adjust the laws that governed it by influencing the lawmakers (although perhaps later and in a much less potent fashion than other businesses). Often these attempts were proactive, suggesting regulations for the future that would work to the advantage of the broadcaster.

In order to influence lawmakers, lobbyists created political action committees (PACs) that provide funds to support politicians with the hope that they, in turn, will create or be supportive of laws favoring the industry the PAC represents.

One of the ironies of free-enterprise big business, it seems, is that it attempts to influence the political system in order to be able to "freely" compete. True "free enterprise" would involve no government intervention, whether beneficial or not. Is such a "hands off" approach to business possible in today's complex society and political system?

One way in which broadcasters are involved in PAC influence is through their concern about the most powerful lobbying force in communications—the telephone companies. A piece of legislation called *telco entry*, which is supported by massive amounts of PAC money from phone companies, would allow the powerful Bell Operating Companies entry into video and audio program delivery, competing directly with the broadcasting industry.

For broadcasters, one strategy in doing battle with the telephone giant is to play its same game—wage a lobbying contest to decide the issue according to who can throw the biggest cash bundle at the politicians. On this battlefield, however, broadcasters are sure to lose when pitted against the monied telephone giants.

Legislators have admitted that on occasion they go looking for revenue sources or additional tax bases from constituencies *that are unrepresented* rather than pursue bills where lobbyists are protecting their best interests.

Case Study 9.6: PACs—To Contribute or Not to Contribute?

You are a broadcaster who must decide whether to heed the pleas of NAB and the state broadcasting association, which are asking you for PAC funds. They want you to contribute for persuasive reasons.

First, the state legislature, hoping to rid political campaigns of mudslinging and negative political commercials, has drawn up a law prohibiting the broadcasting of advertisements if the opponent feels that they contain misstatements of fact. The state broadcasters, with the help of modest PAC funds, inform the legislators that this would violate the federal Communications Act, as well as the First Amendment, and successfully dissuade such legislation.

Second, in order to protect consumers from unscrupulous car salesmen in radio and TV commercials, the state assembly has passed a law specifying that if an auto is advertised for a specific price, it must contain that vehicle's identification number (VIN). The result is that much valuable time in car commercials is taken up with rattling off numerical gibberish. The broadcasters in your state are pushing for repeal of the law and are successful. But they need PAC funds to accomplish the job.

In other ways the broadcasting lobbyists have protected the best interests of your business, enough to make it seem worth it for you to donate to the state broadcasters' PAC, which supported the lobbying and political efforts.

As an entrepreneur who believes deeply in keeping government out of business, however, you are not so sure that such intervention is really the best way of doing things. Your perspective is shaped by having observed government intervention. You have observed that the government has begun to control many aspects of how you do business, from making you put up exit signs in your small station to requiring you to submit employment information about whether your hiring practices meet Equal Employment Opportunity guidelines.

Do you contribute to the PAC funds, conceding that PAC money is needed to work within a system where government policy-making is influenced by PAC-funded lobbyists? Or do you hold fast to your ideals of laissez-faire and withhold your contribution, even though your reluctance could work to your own financial disadvantage? How do your values of integrity come into play here?

REGULATION AND DEREGULATION

As we have seen in previous chapters, when radio began serious news coverage in the 1930s, newspaper publishers feared that radio news would make it impossible for their papers ever again to be the first with a story, since radio could deliver information much more quickly than newspapers. In hindsight, we can only view such fears with a chuckle.

Twenty years later, similar fears arose among radio news operations when television came along and threatened to replace radio as the family's favorite pastime and news source. TV did, in fact, change the fundamental structure and function of radio.

In each case, the existing medium handled the threat by acquiring licenses of the newcomers: "If you can't beat 'em, buy 'em!" Newspaper publishers acquired radio licenses, and later, both newspapers and radio licensees acquired TV licenses.

Today, new and ever-growing technologies again threaten the existence of traditional media. Cable TV has now penetrated most American homes, rivaling free over-the-air television signals. Cable also threatens some radio stations because it can import audio programming by satellite and place it on the cable, diminishing the listening audience of the local radio broadcaster.

At first, cable TV was regulated, much like broadcasting, by the FCC. But in 1984, cable was deregulated. In most markets, this gave cable a monopoly in the kinds of services it provided.

Then, in 1992, cable TV was reregulated. It was required to obtain consent for retransmission of over-the-air signals, even paying for that function. Other regulatory aspects were designed to keep cable from overwhelming broadcasting with its prolific services. Broadcasters fought hard, in their most concerted lobbying effort to date, to have the cable reregulation bill passed, even to the point of trying to override a presidential veto.

In many ways it seems ironic that this should have occurred the decade after broadcasters fought so hard for deregulation of their own business.

Case Study 9.7: Government Intervention, or Hands Off?

Is it inconsistent with any kind of economic philosophy to argue that for one industry, the government should keep its hands off, but for another, it should regulate?

Does it seem "logical" to argue for progressive reform laws when they would benefit an industry, but then argue for the conservative status quo when new laws might be harmful to the industry's best interests? Is it better to be consistent in an ideal or to selectively choose principles that are of the most benefit at the time? Applying principles of ethical reasoning, this becomes a choice between the ideal and the practical, or between Kantian philosophy (always holding to an ideal, no matter what the consequences—see Chapter 2) and situational ethics (following a certain philosophy depending on how beneficial the outcome will be under the specific circumstances).

The media excel at the pragmatic, making applications to profitability that have gained them success and the respect of the world. But to what ideals do the media hold?

To stand back and look at the panorama of this dilemma will bring into view a fundamental conflict in the *business* of U.S. mass media: the progressive nature of new enterprise, of progressive reporting and innovative programming, of entertainment, education, and the arts—versus the conservative status quo of the American capitalistic system, with care not to invest profits wildly in the unknown, and to keep sound, proven business practices.

Some applications of ethical reasoning may seem easy, especially when the reasoning stems from individual value systems. But applying such reasoning to broader economic considerations presents challenges that media entrepreneurs must anticipate.

NOTES

1. Ben Bagdikian, *The Media Monopoly* (Boston: Beacon Press, 1987), as excerpted in Ben Bagdikian, "The Empire Strikes," *Media and Values* (Summer 1989): 4.
2. Norman Lear, "The Culture of Capitalism," *Media & Values* (Summer 1989): 3.
3. These data are taken from "35 Years of Station Transactions," *Broadcasting* (Feb. 13, 1989): 42.
4. Kenneth Blanchard and Norman Vincent Peale, *The Power of Ethical Management* (New York: William Morrow, 1988): 25.
5. Charles Warner and Joseph Buchman, *Broadcast and Cable Selling* (Belmont, Calif.: Wadsworth, 1991).

10

Ethics and Proactive Management

Management policies that can anticipate ethical conflicts and that are visible and known to all the parties involved have been found by experience to function best. They bring about an atmosphere of trust and the image of integrity and ethics. Administrators, staff, and clients alike should be conscious of ethical policies and practices within any organization.

Even so, such policies may still not be responsive to the best interests of all. So what are the characteristics of policies that are ethical and workable?

CHARACTERISTICS OF WORKABLE ETHICAL POLICIES

Proactive

The idea of anticipating ethical dilemmas before they arise is the critical first characteristic of company policy formation. *Proactive* policies are policies that anticipate problems or issues and address them before they become problems. Such proactive policies provide for activating early decision-making on issues involving ethics. They lay out means of carrying out standards that are *positive* in nature and work to avoid problems. These policies are most respected by internal and external publics alike.

Democratically Formulated

Those who are affected by the policies should participate in their formation. Applied theories of public relations, organizational communications, and government advocate the use of ideas from the participants or those who will be governed by the rules. But what if the employees are not conscious of ethical principles or are simply not as ethical as the guidelines ought to provide? Are the elements of an ethical policy to be built on the lowest common denominator? Some observers feel that group efforts reflect higher ideals. The idea of pulling together gives credence to the idea that the whole is greater than the sum of its parts. And many times the policies of collective minds exceed those of the best-intended individuals.

Clarifying Ambiguous Practices

When a practice is *illegal* (that is, when it breaks a law), it obviously should not be exercised, but it nevertheless may be laid out in company policy.[1] When a practice is *legal* but may compromise professional practice or personal integrity, it definitely needs to be articulated. Anticipating the ambiguity and addressing it beforehand prevents headaches later.

Authoritativeness

The best ethical rules go beyond "what the boss says." They are created or endorsed by someone with high authority, but as strikingly important, everyone understands them and agrees to abide by them or suffer the consequences, including job loss. It is this provision of enforcement—a penalty, a consequence or negative effect—that really makes the policy authoritative and gives it clout. However, enforcement of ethics policies is generally difficult. Unlike laws, which have built-in provisions for penalties, sanctions in ethics may be nonexistent, ineffective, or injudiciously applied. Yet professional expectations to abide by the rules may be so strong that they serve as an important check on behavior. Not abiding by the policies can evoke negative reactions from professional peers and may incur a wrath that can have as strong an effect as a harsh sentence. The rules are seen not as something imposed—"do it or else"—but as something that trusted professionals are expected to practice.

General Principles or Values Considered

No rules or laws or set of policies can anticipate all the problems. But if principles incorporate *values,* if they provide for the spirit of the law, not just exact codes for specific situations, then they set forth a tone, a spirit, an atmosphere that can guide more specific conduct. Making ethical decisions often involves not only applying values to professional conduct but deciding which values have higher priority than others. Sometimes two values may have virtue, but behavior will dictate the necessity of choosing one over another. For example, a television account executive whose clients include beer distributors is probably not void of concern about problems of alcohol abuse in our society. But most businesspeople do not want to lose beer and wine advertising revenues. Although one might argue that such advertising does not promote alcoholism, if it is at least part of the problem, which concern has a higher priority? Or if a media salesperson holds to the principle of integrity but also wishes to gain an extra commission by exaggerating the virtues of his or her medium or the reach of its market, which might take priority? To what extent can codes of ethics help here?

Under any ethical policy, managers or employers need to recognize individual employees who are concerned with doing the right thing—those who are honest and have integrity, even at the risk of being overly frank or outspoken. Owners attentive to ethics should respond to remedial voices and encourage criticism in their organizations.

Case Study 10.1: Managing Ethics Policies

Alex, a general manager of a television station in a midsize market, thinks of himself as ethical, a man of integrity. He aspired to his position by his keen ambition, but he did nothing, he thinks, that exceeded proper ethics to get it.

Long before he joined the station, it had large advertising contracts with an automobile dealer who was known for his high-volume sales and hard-sell commercials. Generally, the hard-sell commercials contained exaggerations and improper bait-and-switch ads that customers and the state attorney general's office alike came to recognize as illegal. Upon discovering this, the station's viewers began to associate such advertising practices with the station itself, since it was the exclusive carrier of the commercials. The station was "tainted" by the ads. But the car dealer was the single largest local advertiser for the station and had been for years. Station sales staff understood the problem, but they were reluctant to give up their commissions.

The car dealer has now stopped the illegal activities but continues some of the hard-sell practices that many feel are unethical. His business transactions still lack integrity, and the station still has the stigma of guilt by association. It seems clear that something needs to be done, but what?

Alex tries to convince the dealer to change his commercials so that they will not make insupportable claims but fails. He consults the station's Ethics Guidelines, but they say nothing about accepting advertising from clients with questionable practices. Alex could, of course, simply instruct his sales manager to refuse further advertising from the dealer, even though it would mean some monetary losses to the station (and probably to the dealer as well). Or he could disclaim any wrong practices on the part of the dealer. After all, why should he be on a guilt trip? The station is doing nothing wrong, is it? Yet neither continuing the status quo nor abruptly cutting off the dealer's business seems tenable.

Should Alex go back into the Ethics Guidelines and write something that addresses this problem? If you were in Alex's place, what would you do? What would you tell a staff that is seeking guidance? What would you tell the public, which is looking at the whole affair with a jaundiced eye? Everyone seems to be looking to you for some kind of answer. Perhaps nowhere is leadership more keenly displayed than in such situations.

While in this case it is too late for *proactive policy-making*, some positive proactive work is still possible. This is where Alex shines.

Alex maps out a strategy with the kind of careful planning that has brought him to where he is today. First, he meets personally with the dealer and expresses his concerns. (The dealer professes to have committed no misconduct in his business dealings, of course.) Then he suggests to his news director and assignment editor that an investigative report might help clear the air and determine whether anything is amiss. (Some news people are astounded that Alex would actually encourage such bold, possibly disruptive reporting.) Next, he undertakes a public service campaign that includes on-air public service announcements, ads placed in other media, and recognition of businesses with integrity in special video vignettes placed just after the local newscast. He directs the creation of community task force groups to meet and discuss problems of integrity in business and personal life. The ideas and finds of the task force are written up (at the station's expense) and made available to all local businesses.

The process culminates in successfully swinging the station's previously questionable image to one of integrity and strong business ethics. New clients seek out the station to advertise on its airtime.

Not everyone would approach this case and try to solve its problems the way Alex does. Are his activities what is meant by "ethical leadership in business," or is he simply opportunistic?

In Alex's case, proactive activities relating to the community were triggered by a problem. Other organizations or stations, as a matter of policy, designate a portion of their budget to help promote grassroots solutions to community issues.

A PROACTIVE TV STATION

KIRO-TV, a Bonneville-owned television station in Seattle and a CBS affiliate, boasts a number of successes. In an effort to mobilize community understanding and action, it has helped mount a number of campaigns in recent times.

- *Volunteer Day* was a campaign to recruit volunteers for local nonprofit organizations. Recruiters were allowed to use the station's telephone banks on a Volunteer Day special. An hour-long special, *Local Heroes*, aired spots featuring groups that depend on local volunteers.

- *Hidden Jobs* was an effort to uncover jobs by soliciting information from local businesses on their currently unfilled positions. After running a series in its local news on unemployment, financial planning, alternative careers, and the job market, the station ran a live program that invited businesses to call in with jobs. Information on 1,100 available jobs was provided to job seekers.

- *Crisis in the Workforce* focused on the issue of illiteracy and undereducation in the workforce. Civic and business leaders were brought together in a six-week effort that included a poll to let policy-makers know of community sentiment about such solutions as lengthening the school year and curriculum redesign.

The Seattle station also worked on these issues:

- sheltering the homeless
- collecting food and funds for local food banks
- helping broken families rebuild
- recognizing students who excel
- helping disadvantaged kids get the most out of school
- motivating and encouraging students
- nurturing drug-affected infants
- raising money for the Humane Society and the SPCA
- publicizing its employees' participation in community organizations.

All these activities serve valuable purposes:

1. For the employees, they provide a feeling of individual worth through community service and a sense of participation in community life.
2. They proved to be the most valuable of all the public relations efforts that the station had undertaken. The image of KIRO as a caring organization involved in community concerns became strongly established.
3. The station became visible to businesses, organizations, and publics, which eventually influenced a positive business climate.

KIRO's activities serve as a prototype of proactive policies of ethical practice. In an era and atmosphere when business leaders often grope for ethics or must even seek out what they mean, this TV station embodied proactive ethics in a pragmatic, down-to-earth practice.

Some people will always view such activities as opportunistic or self-serving. It is difficult to change such perspectives. Yet the activities are openly visible for all participants, viewers, clients, and potential clients to see.

Case Study 10.2: Alcohol Advertising

As we saw in Chapter 8, in recent years broadcasting has faced the prospect of losing beer and wine advertising, as it lost tobacco advertising in 1970. Some broadcasters have thought only of the potential economic loss and have fought the proposed ban without regard to its reasons or substance. More thoughtful business leaders have considered what they might do to address the concerns of those fighting alcohol advertising without actually advocating the ban.

Consider the options: How fully and completely can you be an agent for social change—in this case, fight the problems of alcoholism—without harming the free enterprise involved in the advertising of beer and wine?

The Washington State Association of Broadcasters and KOMO-TV, also in Seattle, faced the issue head-on by forming a Broadcasters' Alcohol Task Force. The goals of the task force included the following[2]:

- Provide accurate and current information about alcohol use and abuse.
- Identify approaches to abuse prevention and develop criteria for broadcast materials so that air time would be effectively used for consistent communication on the issue.
- Advise substance abuse experts about the most efficient uses of radio and television.
- Provide an advisory group to assist with research and development of useful materials.
- Work with advertising agencies, breweries, and wineries to help them produce commercials that would discourage the appeal of alcohol consumption by young people ages 15 to 20.

While much of the activity centered on providing materials for use on the air, the task force also provided information about how broadcasters could tie in to community programs already in existence. In order to do this, it conducted extensive research, using focus groups of teens. Four focus groups uncovered the following findings:

- Teenagers believe it is okay to drink but not to drink and drive, although they believe alcohol is a problem.
- Teens are bored, so they turn to alcohol for fun and entertainment.
- Most teens try to have a designated driver.
- Teens are often skeptical of messages of caution in news reports and public service announcements.
- Teens like to hear about proactive solutions (like designating a nondrinking driver) rather than just messages of "don't drink."
- The exposure and frequency of public service announcements could be increased.
- Parents need to educate kids more and increase and encourage involvement.

The teens of the focus groups further suggested the following information be included in public service announcements:

- Show how family and friends are affected by drinking, such as your being killed by a drunk driver and how the driver and his or her family are affected.
- Show statistics of deaths and problems of alcohol, and then say "It's your decision. Don't be a follower—get on with your life. It's your decision, not theirs."
- Use as a statement "If you start drinking, you can lose your license, your respect, your pride, your integrity, your popularity, your body, your mind, your life. Don't drink."
- Use as a statement "Get a life. Have self-respect. Decide what's best for you."
- Use as a statement "Alcohol—it destroys all that's near and dear to you: your family, friendships, and most important, you."
- Have people in local high schools help make commercials. People tend to support what they create.
- Do not tell teens what to do. Give them some options. Show reality.

Using these ideas, the task force encouraged broadcasters to look at their programming and showed them ways to cover the issue, coordinate the sales department, and look at the various aspects of their public service. It also gave helpful suggestions on newsroom policies and strategies for covering the news on related issues. It furnished further national resources for the broadcasters, identified people in the various communities to contact, and suggested some station project ideas.

The project has received national recognition for its innovations in tackling a problem without partisan dogmatism. The work may have fended off legislative action moving toward the outright banning of beer and wine advertising from radio and TV.

The lesson from all this? Broadcasters can practice ethics and strikingly demonstrate proactive business leadership. Learning about the values of other perspectives in facing the advertising and economic dilemmas of the profession may not be a bad place to start.

RULES AND REGULATIONS

Perhaps no business is plagued more by bureaucratic rules and regulations than the broadcasting and telecommunications industries. Since the FCC has imposed increasingly more regulations, some associated business leaders have cried out against the regulation of free enterprise. They have fought in any number of ways against restrictions as such, often polarizing the setting by insisting on nothing short of the complete elimination of rules and regulations.

Although the 1980s were marked by FCC deregulations and a pro-business Reagan administration, nevertheless many rules have remained: for political advertising, the Section 315 "equal time" provision for political candidates; equal employment practices; the demands of the Occupational Safety and Health Administration (OSHA); business taxes; employment taxes; advertising controls; and scores of state and local regulations. Even the most carefully designed lobbying has not been successful in removing more than its fair share of regulations.

The situation seems to be here to stay. Facing hundreds of regulations, small-business and "Ma and Pa" stations are at a distinct disadvantage. Often they do not know what the rules are or how their expectations can best be met in business practices. Where can they get help? What they cannot do individually, they might achieve on a collective basis. Broadcasters, for instance, can affiliate with their respective state broadcasting associations or other professional organizations that offer collective solutions to many of these dilemmas.

Political Advertising

Problem:

Political advertising on radio and television is highly regulated by federal law. Because candidates themselves are ignorant of or simply overlook many legal requirements, requests for ads are not suitably placed or properly produced.

Solution:

Some state associations have produced small booklets or guidelines for political candidate advertising on radio and TV. They contain the basics of what a broadcaster is expected to know, including definitions from the law itself. They also contain information helpful to affiliated businesses, such as advertising agencies. What about sales and commercial practices? They're there too. In addition, state associations often sponsor seminars that may include representatives from both government and industry.

Information

Problem:

How is a broadcaster to know the fine points of general laws and regulations? What if a listener threatens legal action or makes some demand under the guise of legal rights? Many smaller broadcasters really cannot afford to retain legal counsel, even to scare off small threats.

Solution:

Offer a legal hotline through your professional association. Many stations can band together for a common legal counsel (as many state associations do) and get good advice in a way that a single business person could not afford.

Hotlines are available to members of the National Association of Broadcasters (NAB) and at the Reporters' Freedom of Information Center and consumer affairs offices in various states. Solutions may be found by calling the government offices involved (like the FCC, the Federal Trade Commission, the Internal Revenue Service).

Deadlines

Problem:

Like a sword hanging overhead, there are always filing deadlines that broadcasters must meet. Even the best business leader can miss out on some of the continuous submission of paperwork that is required. Penalties, usually monetary, can hurt, especially for a small business.

Solution:

One could make a calendar of all the deadlines and systematically keep track of them that way. Professional organizations sometimes do this as part of their services. The Washington State Association of Broadcasters, for example, offers a Calendar of Broadcaster Events and Deadlines.

Employment Applications

Problem:

Every month, broadcasters receive dozens of unsolicited employment applications from qualified (and unqualified) persons wanting to work in the business. Simply recognizing and responding to applications takes more time than it is worth. When the broadcaster finally does need a new employee, the task of sorting through the submitted resumes to find the right person can be overwhelming. So there is a double problem of handling applications and finding just the right person for a position when a vacancy occurs.

Solution:

Professional organizations often keep a job bank—a kind of mini–employment agency. Sometimes they maintain two banks, one for employment applications and one for employers' help-wanted announcements. A job bank can furnish a defined, classified, or screened set of applications to an employer, and provide a listing of available positions to job-seekers, perhaps for a nominal fee.

Finding Qualified Minorities

Problem:

Even with the best intentions to be responsive to affirmative action, sometimes a station may find no qualified minorities in the pool of applicants.

Solution:

There are several ways of attacking this problem.

1. Broadcasters can support the education and training of minorities by providing for *minority scholarships* at schools and universities. This may be more than the pursestrings of an individual business can afford, but if done collectively, it becomes workable and an important function of a professional organization.

2. Broadcasters can provide *in-house training programs* for minorities. Some businesses are convinced that if they want to get the right people to work for their organization, they must shape and mold them themselves. Start with a minority youth or someone else from a pool of applicants who may not be as fully qualified as you would like. Develop an apprentice program in which the new employee works closely with current staff in a temporary position. If things work out through a probationary period, a qualified employee is the result. If not, repeat the process. The understanding from the outset must be that the work situation is on a trial basis, pending the development of important characteristics like responsibility and integrity.

3. Offer a *minority internship* to a student majoring in journalism where an empty position exists. Sometimes, competition for such internships can be intense, especially for minority students, so incentives such as *paid internships* may elicit the most promising interns. Usually the pay is minimal, since these are college students earning college credit. In most cases, in order not to violate labor practices, the intern *must* earn legitimate college credit for his or her labor.

Sources of New Ideas

Problem:

Businesses of the same nature have to confront the same kinds of problems. Different businesses arrive at different solutions and come up with a variety of ideas for addressing these problems. Other businesses are often very interested in learning how others have handled these matters.

Solution:

A good arena for sharing ideas is, again, the professional association, which often offers:

- Conferences, where meetings of good minds can share worthwhile ideas
- Newsletters, in which timely information can be disseminated to association members
- Aggressive, proactive businesses, which make contact with other businesses and seek out new ideas on their own initiative.

Following Legislation

Problem:

When news bills are introduced into Congress or a state legislature, business leaders need to know about these and know how to voice a position on such bills.

Solution:

Be part of a lobby! This is one of the main functions of many professional organizations. While not all lobbying practices are sound, there are laws to keep such practices in check. The collective voice from such organizations can be the most striking way that constituents can make themselves heard in a democracy.

Public Service Announcements

Problem:

Many constituents in a broadcasting community or market work with legitimate nonprofit causes or general organizational issues and ask broadcasting stations to run public service announcements (PSAs). Not even a station with the best of intentions can meet all the requests—there are simply not enough available time slots into which deserving PSAs can be placed. A station receives no pay for running a PSA spot.

Solution:

Some state broadcasters' associations have programs known as non-commercial sustaining announcements (NCSAs). Available spots are provided by agreement with the state association, which acts as administrator or coordinator and receives a nominal fee for guaranteed placement. One state broadcasters' association helped the state public health department in campaigns to increase awareness of infant mortality issues, the dangers of cigarette smoking, and AIDS prevention. It also helped promote small businesses and informed the public about options for job skills training. In so doing, it provided important public services while saving some operating expenses.

One may argue that broadcasters have a keen responsibility to provide such services without charge—after all, the "airwaves belong to the public" and ought to be used for the public good. This in itself appears to pose an ethical issue. However, given the high demand for PSAs, which exceeds the ability of stations to supply, some systematic screening must occur. The state broadcasters' association, able to service and work with its members, acts as a screening and coordinating agency and provides a service that is worth its commission.

A BUSINESS ETHICS SELF-QUIZ

Completing the following quiz will help you analyze your own position as it relates to business values and ethical practices. Write down your answer for each question on a sheet of paper. If no one single choice seems to be best, pick the closest choice. At the end of the quiz, figure your score and interpret your results.

1. The essence of my interest in broadcasting is:
    (a) to make money for the owners and stockholders
    (b) to make as much money as I can for myself

    (c) to serve my community and the public

    (d) to work in a marketplace where the public profits from our service, and we profit from the business of serving

    (e) to offer entertainment, escape, and pleasure for listeners to help them endure otherwise dreary lives

2. The nature of my ideal listener is:

    (a) someone intelligent and alert, ready to receive new information and be challenged by new entertainment

    (b) a potential consumer of products and services advertised on my station, someone I can help consume better

    (c) someone whom I can mold—to like my entertainment, to be convinced by the ideas communicated over my station

    (d) someone who has invited my station as a guest into their room, car, and is hosting my station

    (e) a slob sitting back in his underwear and sucking on a can of beer—a tiny piece of data in the large system of numbers and ratings

3. Generally, my station best serves my audience when:

    (a) its profits are maximized so that there can be better talent, programs, creativity, and equipment

    (b) it reinvests revenues back into community-oriented public service programming

    (c) its programming caters to whatever is popular, what the audience wants, regardless of its nature, weirdness, or taste

    (d) it serves as a friend to the lonely and isolated, as a one-on-one medium

    (e) it creates an image with which the listener identifies, regardless of what is programmed, to retain the listener at rating time

4. If a good advertiser protested one of my programs and my sales manager wanted to remove the program, but my program director wanted to keep it, to whom would I listen?

    (a) My sales manager

    (b) My program director

    (c) I would not intervene but let them fight it out and the "winner" decides

    (d) I would call in outside help to solve the problem

    (e) I would carefully think about it and make my own decision, regardless of whom I may alienate

5. My station programs primarily to a younger audience, with a large proportion of teens. A beer distributor wants to advertise during the time when my audience comprises mostly teens. Do I run his ads during these times?
   (a) Yes, my station needs all the revenues it can get.
   (b) Yes, because there has been no evidence of a causal relationship between advertising and alcohol abuse.
   (c) Yes, but I would run some alcohol abuse PSAs during those times too.
   (d) No, but I would try to persuade my advertiser to use other time slots.
   (e) No, I don't want to carry beer ads on my youth-oriented station.

6. I have a chance to boost my ratings by carrying an infamous "shock jock" who uses questionable material that borders on indecency. Do I use him?
   (a) Yes, higher ratings mean higher profits and more money in my pocket.
   (b) Yes, my audience doesn't mind such material.
   (c) Yes, social mores have changed, making such material okay today.
   (d) No, such material might put my station in jeopardy with FCC policies.
   (e) No, my listeners probably wouldn't complain, but I personally object to such material.

7. In hiring someone for an important middle-management position, I have an application from a qualified white male with a proven track record, and one from a minority who has no proven track record and may be less qualified. Whom do I choose?
   (a) The more qualified, regardless of any other factor
   (b) The white male, since it would be easier to work with him
   (c) The minority, because I need to satisfy affirmative action demands
   (d) The minority, because I believe in equality and the need to allow minorities to gain access to higher positions in broadcasting
   (e) The minority, since it would be easier to work with him

8. My station is popular because of its "more music, less talk" format. I can only get so much money per advertising spot in this market, but advertising demands are rising and I need to

carve out more available time slots for them. But that might lower my ratings. What do I do?

(a) Take the chance to run more spots—I need the revenue.

(b) Keep the format as is—I can get by with the status quo.

(c) Increase the number of spots just a little; maybe no one will notice.

(d) Change the format—get more clients, carve out many more available slots for ads.

(e) Keep the "more music" format and increase the rate card anyway—I won't follow the market for rates but set the trend!

9. As a TV station manager, I am approached by a promoter who offers to sell me a promotion package that includes some suspicious "prizes." The promotion would give great visibility to my station. But because of the unknown nature of the prizes, I'm not sure the whole thing won't backfire on me. What do I do?

(a) Take the chance—the probable boost in ratings will be worth it.

(b) Resist the offer—the station's reputation could be hurt more than enhanced.

(c) Take the offer but insist on checking everything to ensure there is no problem.

(d) Take the offer, and if anything goes wrong, blame the promoter.

(e) Get as much information as I can about the promotion, but don't buy it—just use the promoter's ideas.

10. My sales manager, a good friend with whom I've worked for years, has falsified affidavits for the commercials that our station is supposed to have run but didn't. What do I do?

(a) Admit the problem, despite the bad publicity, since at least I'm being honest.

(b) Admit the problem, blame it on my sales manager, fire her, and claim the station is now clean.

(c) Hide the problem, since no one will ever know except she and I.

(d) Punish the sales manager, keep the problem low profile, and offer my clients "goodwill" packages, even if they don't understand the real reason why.

(e) Quit—get out of the station before the whole thing explodes.

Scoring the Self-Quiz

Give yourself the following number of points for your choices in the ten questions:

						Your Points
1:	a-5	b-3	c-8	d-5	e-1	_____
2:	a-8	b-5	c-1	d-7	e-0	_____
3:	a-2	b-4	c-3	d-8	e-2	_____
4:	a-2	b-4	c-1	d-1	e-8	_____
5:	a-1	b-3	c-4	d-6	e-7	_____
6:	a-1	b-3	c-4	d-7	e-8	_____
7:	a-3	b-1	c-5	d-7	e-4	_____
8:	a-3	b-3	c-5	d-3	e-7	_____
9:	a-2	b-5	c-6	d-0	e-0	_____
10:	a-10	b-4	c-0	d-1	e-0	_____
				Your Total:		_____

What Your Total Means

10 to 25 points:

Your ethics are economic existential. Making money is probably foremost in your life and your transactions with others. You live life in a very practical hard-nosed manner in order to derive the most pleasure from it.

26 to 40 points:

Your ethics are utilitarian and pragmatic. Your work centers on convenience, compromise, and practicality, where you try for the best solution for the most people.

41 to 60 points:

Your ethics are principle-centered idealism. Regardless of tough consequences, you always intend to use your values in your decision-making.

61 to 78 points:

Your ethics are altruistic and other-centered. Compassion and consideration of other people's feelings often play an important role in your decision-making.

Note that the numbering system and the meaning of the totals given here are not necessarily an accurate indication of your ethical philosophy. Now that you know about the four ethics systems, you may wish to go back and see how your answer to each of the ten questions reveals your system of ethics more accurately.

Thinking About Your Choices

There are no "right" answers to the self-quiz, only choices. But there are some observations you might make about yourself concerning the choices you made.

1. Did you choose your responses honestly—the way you really feel? Or did you respond in a way that you'd like someone else to think is the way you do things? Integrity is often a desirable characteristic in ethical practices—making decisions on the basis of your own value system.

2. If your answers were honest, do they accurately reflect the kind of person you are, as well as the kind of business person you really want to be? Do values that you consider important (perhaps "responsibility," "compassion," "loyalty," "honesty") come through in your answers? Or do they belie what you really are on the inside?

3. Where do you draw the line between your obligations (what you are bound to do by company policy or by law) and your freedom to act according to your system of ethics? Do you prefer to be guided in all your decisions by policies and law, or would you rather make hard decisions and be blamed or praised for the consequences?

4. Where you have latitude in making decisions, do you have a predetermined set of personal principles upon which you base your decisions, or do you prefer situational ethics, making decisions according to circumstances at the time?

5. Does your own set of values allow you the quality of life you desire? Are your means taking you to the ends you wish to achieve? If not, what is your strategy for developing characteristics or values that lead you on the path you wish to go?

The examination of ethics in broadcasting and telecommunications is based upon the same premise that guides the study of ethics in every profession and in every life: As Plato first said it, "The unexamined life is not worth living."

The goal and aim of this book and especially this chapter have been to promote and induce that self-examination in you. Much of our society gropes in search of identifying the values essential to a productive life. If anyone ought to have firm notions of the value system under which he or she operates, it must be workers and managers in broadcasting and telecommunications—those who have much to do with shaping the way we see things and the way we think. It is to this end that this book is dedicated.

NOTES

1. For example, Dow Jones and Company has published a "Conflicts of Interest Policy." Some of these policies address practices of illegal activities like "insider trading." For example: "Each employee is expected to bend over backwards to avoid any action, no matter how well-intentioned, that could provide grounds for suspicion . . . that the writing of a news story or item or scheduling of advertising was influenced by a desire to affect the stock's prices."
2. The information that follows is from *Tough Choices: Tackling the Teen Alcohol Problem*, a Community Outreach Handbook (Seattle: Washington State Association of Broadcasters—Alcohol Task Force, 1991).

Index